clockwise from top left:
TIFFANY DASH
GINA JACKSON
CATHERINE 'CAT' RUSSELL
LIBBY PAPIAN
JASMINE JONES

clockwise from top left:
DEWAIN MEEKS
ALEXIS FAYNE
AMANDA ELLIOTT
IMANI WILLIAMS
MARVIN BELL II

clockwise from top left:
ALEXIS MAXINE MARIE
JAMERISON, TASHA MCCULLER
ERIC OLIVER, ASHLEY POLK
NELSON DORVLO

clockwise from top left:
KENNETH CLARK
TANNER SENTER
DEJÁ CHERRELLE WHITE
CHRIS 'WOODIE' FARRAR
BRIANNA BARNES

clockwise from top left:
JANAE BROTHERS, OLACHI ANAEMEREIBE
JASMINE 'JJ' JONES, ALICIA CASTILLO
AYRIEL HADLEY

clockwise from top left:
DEVON L. SMALL
JEQUETTA SMITH
KADIJIA HAYES
KARISSA ANDERSON
LAUREN WALKER

clockwise from top left:
RANEISHA WILLIAMS
BRIANA PEPPERS
DENIECE CHATMAN
MISHA FOSTER

clockwise from top left:
CHRIS WILLIAMS
BOBBIE JEAN BARNETT
LARRY MALONE
MIKE JONES

StudioStL

Self-portraits written by the students of College Bound

NUMBER 1

Foreword by ISAAC BRUCE

Published by

Studio StL

This book is a publication of StudioSTL, a literary arts center for students and community. We gratefully acknowledge the staff of 826 Valencia, who inspired this work and offered guidance.
www.studiostl.org/info@studiostl.org

Special thanks to College Bound, www.collegeboundstl.org

The student authors of College Bound attend Clyde C. Miller Career Academy and University City High School in St. Louis where the students met for writing and editing sessions with the StudioStL volunteer writing staff. StudioStL empowers kids, 6 to 18, by helping them discover, develop and celebrate their individual voices through writing. We believe a literary toolbox and writing skills – whether for fun, for school, in personal or professional life – are indispensable lifelong gifts. We bring together writers, artists, and educators to work with students on writing projects that are kid-friendly, but also help build writing skills. Best of all, because we rely 100% on trained volunteers to work with our students, we are able to offer free student programming, which we hope keeps them coming back for more.

Published June 2007, by StudioStL
Copyright © 2007 by StudioStL
All rights reserved by StudioStL and the authors
ISBN 978-0-9795112-0-2

Editor: Julie Dill
Copyediting: Leslie Evans
Managing Editors: Karissa Anderson, Clyde C. Miller Academy
Ayriel Hadley, University City High School

Student Editorial Staff: Karissa Anderson, Brianna Barnes, Janae Brothers, Deniece Chatman, Kenneth Clark, Tiffany Dash, Alexis Fayne, Kadijia Hayes, Alexis Jamerison, J.J. Jones, Eric Oliver, Tanner Senter, Jequetta Smith, Dejá White

Photography copyright © 2007 by LappinVogler Photography
www.lappinvogler.com.

Book Design & Production: Ken Botnick & Mason Miller,
emdash Studio, St. Louis, Missouri

Printed in United States by Edwards Brothers, Ann Arbor, Michigan

1) 978-0-9795112-0-2

Contents

Foreword

They told me I was too slow.

Many of my friends, my relatives, my coaches – they told me I'd never become a starter on my high school team. I'd never go to college. I most certainly would never realize my dream to become a professional football player.

I was too slow.

And though I did become a starter at Dillard High (all-city and state 5A champion 1989), and did go to college (Memphis University) and did go on to play professional football (a second round draft choice in 1994) and now have over 13,000 career receiving yards and 80 touchdown passes, including the game winner in Super Bowl XXXIV, they were right in one sense.

I was too slow. I was too slow to pick up a book when I was in high school, so focused was I on playing football. I was too slow to read my Bible, though it was the very first book my mother put in my hands as a child. I was too slow to listen to the great advice that I got from my teachers, my preachers, my coaches and all the people who loved me when they said, there's more to life than football.

It was long after I left my inner city neighborhood in Fort Lauderdale, Fla., attended college and became a star football player that I found my purpose in life – to help others find their way and to give glory to God.

I believe the path begins with reading and writing. You can get started now by turning the pages of this wonderful anthology. It's filled with wisdom from high school students who were faster than I was when it comes to getting a leg up on life.

They've done a lot of reading and studying through a program called College Bound that has put them on a path to academic success. And with the commitment of StudioSTL, a writing and mentoring program, they've found their voices and written some stories. Their accounts are by turns witty and poignant, intelligent and emotional, joyful and, in some cases, angry.

It's the anger that really catches my attention. So many of the students heard what I heard when I was growing up in Fort Lauderdale. They were the voices that said in so many words, "You'll never amount to anything..." Or as mentioned before, "You're too slow."

When I was young I had my way of dealing with those voices. I loved playing football so much that there wasn't anything anyone could say that would stop me. So I blocked out the voices and used whatever anger I felt was rocket fuel for my dream. And when it was clear that I really did need to get faster, I learned how to do it. I got on a proper diet, lifted weights, and ran intervals and sprints. I ran a 4.8 40-yard dash in high school. By the time I was drafted I could do a 4.53 and most people say I'm even faster in a game situation with the ball in my hands and the end zone beckoning.

You might say I was obsessed. So obsessed that I didn't study very hard and I failed to get the scores necessary to get into a four-year university where I could play football my freshman year.

But that didn't stop me. With my high school coach's help I got admitted to a junior college in California. Yet there was one more obstacle: money. I needed $300 to get to California and my family didn't have it. I mowed lawns, but there weren't enough real lawns in my hardscrabble neighborhood – just the church lawn. Finally, my mother, through prayer and sacrifice, saved enough money for me to add to what little I had. And off I went to prove God's word in me.

I had great success on the football field and I made a lot of money. But here's what I learned about money. It only makes you more of who you already are. And what I was a few years ago was simply a decent man and a very good football player.

But not long after that Super Bowl season in 2000, I began to follow my heart. It took me back to that first book that I held in my hands: the Bible. I read it again and again... and other books, too, that speak of faith and commitment. Soon I found peace and a purpose.

One of my favorite Bible passages is from Corinthians... and it speaks to the anger that all of us sometimes feel when people tell us that we can't have what we want out of life. It's a passage I'd like to share with the students who wrote the wonderful narratives for this anthology and with you.

Love is patient, love is kind. It does not envy, it does not boast, it is not proud. It is not rude, it is not self-seeking, it is not easily angered, it keeps no record of wrongs. Love does not delight in evil but rejoices with the truth. It always protects, always trusts, always hopes, always perseveres.

What this passage tells me is that it's not enough to simply forgive those people who doubt you ... those who might have said you were too slow. Forgiving also means forgetting.

It's time to replace anger with love. In doing so, we can make a better world for those around us and those yet to come.

Love never fails.

Isaac Bruce
February, 2007

Birdstory

Birds are the strangest yet most beautiful creatures. One day I was walking to the grocery store with my mom and this bird (a pigeon at that!) was flying toward me. Before I knew it, it was no more than a foot away from my face. I was so scared, but I guess it finally opened its eyes, took a quick left, and disappeared. I know I just stood there like, "What just happened? Did you not see me?" Seconds later, though, I had to laugh about it. No big deal.

You know, it's just how swift and smooth birds are that makes me nervous. The spinning of an owl's head; the length of an eagle's wing; and the evil appearance of a crow. The odd thing is that if I were an animal, I would love to be a bird. I know it's weird, but I have my reasons.

I would love to fly and be able to soar over the world and feel the wind in my face. If I could do this, I would figure out all the secrets going on and try to reveal the truth. There are people with this golden power, but I doubt they will ever be brave enough to show and tell. The point is that I would have proof of what is going on and then I would change lives.

That's how I feel when I think about my future. I know I've got what it takes to be successful, to spread my wings and soar high, to fly wherever I want, to be as wise as an owl. But sometimes I'm still scared that in the end it won't happen.

Another fear I have is not living up to my potential and just settling for less. I fear not taking advantage of everything in front of me. It seems like every other day when I ride the bus I hear old friends, now middle-aged, catching up on the days when they were "hot." They're saying things like, "Man, I'm just now getting my act together, if only I knew then what I know now." I have heard that so many times it is just stuck in my head. I don't want to end up that way ever, because I would feel like I have wasted my time and my life.

I don't want to have tons of regrets when I'm grown and ponder on what I should've or could've done. And I guess that's where the birds come into play for me. They have all the freedom to explore and find out what they want to know. They can take a day and find out these things, whereas I have to wait my turn. I know I have potential, but I don't know what's all out there for me. Being a bird would let me spread my wings and figure out all the facts of life in a day.

I have many advantages in my life and not progressing to my best would be a shame, so I fear not pursuing my dreams. But in a way, the people on the bus are a sort of motivation and kind of a reality check. Hearing them keeps me focused and gives me insight as to how people in their shoes feel. And, to me, that would feel like a huge regret. I would feel like I let myself and my family down. The people who have ever influenced me or taught me – I would feel like I let them down. I don't feel like I'm not going to be successful, but if I were not that would ruin me and make me feel like I didn't give my all and all the work I have done is useless.

After all, I only have one life to live, so I don't want it to go to waste when there are opportunities left and right that can take me to where I want to go. That's why birds are beautiful creatures to me.

Inside Libby

At first when I was asked what I wanted to write about, I really didn't know what I wanted write. I think I was overanalyzing the whole assignment. During one of the College Bound meetings, Beth brought up the point of me being tired. So I started writing about sleeping. But while I was writing about sleeping, I realized it wasn't something I really felt strongly about. So one of my friends suggested that I write about something that I do have strong feelings about. So I started thinking and I came up with something. It's a personal subject, but I decided to write about it anyway.

It all started when I was born. I was born in a hospital in N. Philly. I only weighed about three pounds (I was a preemie). My mother, Chevelle Williams, decided to give me up for adoption. I never got the chance to know my birth mother. I was adopted a few weeks later (when I was up to weight) by my mother, Amy Papian. A month or two later we flew home here to St. Louis. The rest is history, but that's the basics.

But, because I was adopted I've felt that something was wrong with me because my mother didn't keep me. I've always wondered why. My birth mother had a child a year before I was born, my brother, and she kept him. So it made me think why didn't she keep me? I always figured that it was since she was only eighteen with two kids, wasn't married and still living with her mother. I think that her mother (my grandmother) made her give me up for adoption because she felt that two kids was too much. Also I feel that maybe she felt that she would be stuck taking care of me and my brother. So she just thought it would be better to give me up, but this is just what I think. It's not what I know.

Ever since then I've just felt that something was wrong with me. That's why sometimes when my friends or someone close to me gets mad or doesn't want to talk to me, I feel like there's something wrong with me. But, it's just because I feel like I'm not good enough to be their friend. Sometimes I feel like this even with my family members. For example, if I do something wrong, even if it's something little, I feel like I'm not a good person or daughter or sister. And, I hate to be alone, so I try so hard to keep friends and family close to me.

7

I feel that these feelings tie into the fact that I have low self-esteem sometimes.

When I was in middle school it was worse than it is now because then I really cared about what everybody thought. In middle school I had glasses and braces, and I was quiet around my friends and I didn't talk a lot.

But the problem is still there. I realize this when people say how nice I am and my reply is simply, "Oh, for real? You think so?" I never really acknowledge the good things about myself. Maybe it's because I don't believe they're true. Also I always seem to compare myself to others instead of being happy with me. It's weird because it's not like this every day. Some days it's the exact opposite and I think highly of myself and don't feel that I'm not cute.

I think my low self-esteem comes from the fact that I feel like there's something wrong with me, and also because when I was younger, other African-American children told me that I was ugly because I was dark-skinned. Even though that was the past and time has changed, those words have stuck with me. But, I feel that I'm getting better because I have fewer days when I feel down and low. For me it really helps when I talk to people about how I'm feeling. I sometimes even find out that I'm not the only one. This makes me feel a lot better.

I'm going to continue to work on this problem and try to keep a positive attitude and eventually this feeling will go away. I'm personally lucky enough to have friends and family that care about me. That will help me along the way. It's not going to be easy, but I believe I can do it.

Bullets Don't Have Eyes

"When are we going to die?" My younger bro asked me this. A seven year old boy asked me, teary-eyed, "When are we going to die?" I sat there for a moment, stunned, speechless. How do you tell a child younger than you when he will die? It reminded me of the time when my family and I were watching T.V. Bush was talking about the war and again my brother asked, "When will it be over?" I told him, "In like ten minutes." He said "No, the war."

Some go unseen, unheard, and untouched by the outside world, but me, I live one everyday, a war. Over the years I have lost many friends to gang and gun violence. Many people think that is an overstatement, not knowing where I come from. Walnut Park, or as they call it Lil' Vietnam, is said to be the worst place in St. Louis, which in some terms may make it the most dangerous place in the country. Killing happens here almost every week, but until two years ago, when I was fourteen, it never hit close to home.

My close friend Nick's cousin was killed in a drive-by shooting last year and it made me think about the saying "Here today, gone tomorrow." I was just talking to him on the very corner of his death. We were laughing and joking the day before. That next day when I came home, Nick came over and I found out. It was hard for him to tell me, but it was also hard for me to hear it.

About a week later coming home from school, I saw more than the usual amount of people on the street. Thinking nothing of it, I walked into the house. The news came on, top story, "...the victim of the shooting last night at Goodfellow and Floyd has passed away, his name is not released. Police say he was shot three times in the back and once in the chest. The other teen with him is still in critical condition." As the story ended, the phone began to ring.

"Devon, have you heard?" said a low, light, monotone voice.

"Heard what?" I asked.

"Sword was shot; he passed this morning." the voice answered.

"Goddamn, I'm gon' call you back."

I ran down the street to confirm the news. It was true. My oldest girl cousin was dating him. I had to call to break the news to her. I told my grandma, and around here when someone is killed we know to stay away from the windows and to go outside for as little time as possible. Even though it might be a regular, normal set of events, deaths like this will never be normal. Just because we have become accustomed to them, does not mean we will get used to them.

But, the hardest loss I've had to cope with was the death of the only positive male figure in my life, my grandfather. He lost his life to cancer in 2006; this by far is the hardest, not just for me, but for my grandma also. She was down, which in turn broke me down, but I couldn't show too much emotion because I had to be her backbone. I had to help her get through it. Ever since then I had to become the man of the house, I have to be the leader for my little brother, and sometimes big brother. This gave me the reason why I didn't join a gang; I never wanted to get involved it because I knew in the back of my mind that if I did I would somehow make them think it was okay.

Like any other teen I've had my share of bad decisions and trouble, some more dangerous than others, somehow I find my way out of it. Me knowing that I can come home and be safe, safe as I can be, that's the reason I try to do something with my life, rather than to fall victim to the ghetto. If my grandpa taught me one thing it was to be something.

I realize the things we think we know are not written in stone. Our lives can anytime change, in a blink of an eye. Death is a part of life and no one really knows when it will come on to you. When you ask a grown up, the answer will be, "when God is ready for you." The fact is that after years of terror and violence, I have never been scared. I feel like because "I'm from here" I can't get hurt, not considering what little protection that provides. Bullets don't have eyes.

She Looks On

A teenage girl
too curious for her own good
comes across a mirror
a magical mirror reflecting
back.

A young girl
barely the age of seven
in the living room of a beautiful home
playing Monopoly with her mother and brothers
laughing, joking, smiling
She looks on...

She sits on her porch
with her brothers
suitcases and plastic bags next to them
in a large mound
she cries and they comfort
while her mother walks out
the pink eviction notice in her mother's hand.
She looks on...

The family together again
now in an apartment
kids play cards on the kitchen table
while mother cooks
joking, happy
as in their beautiful home
She looks on...

In a building
mother sits on a bench
her head down

tears roll down from her eyes
the young girl screams
please! don't leave me here!
She looks on...

A woman pulls her down the hall
she remembers this moment
like yesterday
taken from her mother
as hurtful as it is for her
Still, she looks on...

A strange home
with four other children
a woman she has just met
a foster home
she is nine by this time
she dials her brother's number
no answer
she puts down the phone
leans against the wall
tears in her eyes
She looks on...

She hugs her grandmother
her brother smiles
she smiles
I missed you guys
her brother jokes and sings
reunited and it feels so good
they look happy
one thing is missing
her mother
She looks on...

It's strange with her grandmother
they are very distant
her grandmother yells
you are just like your mom
the young girl thinks to herself
why is that a bad thing
She looks on...

She sits in her room
all alone, quiet
things are different now
she starts to feel uneasy
like the calm before the storm
Still, she looks on...

Then it happens
she sees the girl and her grandmother
arguing
it looks serious
she picks up the phone
shortly after
suitcases appear again
She looks on...

Another new home
unfamiliar territory
yet still with family
her dad's grandmother
she should be happy
but things only seem worse
her world turns black
She looks on...

The young girl is fragile
a bad attitude
temper is quick
grades are dropping
she is trying new things
not necessarily good
she's at the bottom of the hole
She looks on...

At school she goes to a meeting
a new program opportunity
she thinks to herself
who chose me?
who believes in me?
she starts to feel hope
maybe she can climb out of the hole
She looks on...

13

She gets a call
from a friend
"I'm in" her friend exclaims
the young girl is excited for her friend
yet disappointed
she looks for the director's phone number
she calls, but no answer
maybe just maybe
She looks on...

She soon gets another phone call
from the director
the director talks to her
there is a situation
her grades are terrible
yet the woman didn't tell her "no"
she believes in this girl
this helps
the young girl starts to believe in herself
they set up a meeting
She looks on...

The teenage girl smiles
she remembers the meeting
during summer at school
the long walk down the hall
the woman's delicate frame
great smile
her strong embrace
her encouraging words
she needed that
she knew this woman could change her
give her the push
it becomes reality
She looks on...

The young girl continues to look
but the image is different
it's no longer the past, but the present
smiling and happy
good grades and a job
full of opportunities

yet the past still holds her back
she often thinks
how things could have been
should have been
but in the same moment
she is happy
She looks on...
Suddenly, the mirror changes
it's normal again
and she sees her reflection
she realizes what has just happened
even though she went through
many ups and downs
with help
she overcame it
she is in a better place in life
she should take advantage of it
and she will
she looked at her reflection
smiled, and proudly said,
"I am proud to be Tiffany Dash."

My Demon

Cold breathing on the back of my neck
Leaving painful feelings I'll never forget
To pray to a GOD
And ask Him to relieve me
Is impossible when the people I trust the most won't believe me.
Fingernails scraping the board
What did I do, what are you here for?
Stop whispering softly in my ears
You. Leave me alone, why are you here?
Jump. Why should I? It's all pointless to me.
Jump. I'm not listening, please get away from me.
I won't kill myself and no, I won't hurt me either
I'll break your voice and sweat you out like a fever.
My Demon, my inner self I've learned are both different.
But you're mad and crazy just like a hit man or villain.
You find yourself comforted in the pain of someone else
You'll keep eating and eating until there's no one left.
In your little head someone's eating at you
And now you're the one feeling a little confused.
You're no longer My Demon I've grown out of you finally.
As much as I choose to let you alone
I hear your voice nightly.
You picked at me like a sore
And I think that you should go
My mind and brain are sore
And I refuse to deal with you anymore
You're no longer My Demon!

My Pulse

mY PuLsE is the result
why muh day wasn't well
it couldnt be tha reason it was swell
mY PuLsE is the result of hours blown off
it's not tha reason i cough
but mayb the reason im so lost.
mY PuLsE is the result
of a life changin impact
tha changed me from Catherine to Cat
to make me wish i could go baq
and change it all
mY PuLsE is the result
im here today with a lot of my mind
and the reason i can find the time
to let it all out and let my self shine.
if your pulse is the result
ur life keeps on changin
then jus keep on hangin
cuz ur pulse will soon b ur own
mY PuLsE is the result
i have the adrenaline to write
what's right and fight
the fight that darkens my night
mY PuLsE is the result
of my voice bein loud
helping take away peoples dark clouds
and maqin my moms proud
mY PuLsE is the result
of the freedom of speech
that i attempt to reach

over all heartaches that creep.
that i may hav to breach.
iS uR PuLsE the result
u act tha way u do
makin me sick like the flu
and causin me to refuse
all the things i chose to do wit u
iS uR PuLsE the result
of me writin these words
to make sure im heard
from the catepillars to the birds
iS OuR PuLsEthe result
of this endin conclusion
dead dim dying conclusion
to the truth that it is what it is.
i know that My pulse is the result
i can smile like i do
change my ways and attitude
and to chose not to be rude
to my enemies and cruel
my pulse is the result
that i can say hello to you
wave and make you say
"hey today's a beautiful day."
the result of that pulse
is that if i can change
u can rearrange yourself
merely step out of self
to make our pulses
beat in tune!

Truth & Honesty

"Oh my God. Look at her hair."

"Guess what I heard...."

"Didn't she wear that last week?"

These are some of the comments people say after they have just given a person a compliment. I know what you're thinking: they are so fake! But, Jequetta, didn't you just do that today? Oh hell. I didn't want to be honest that would have hurt his feelings.

So, today at lunch, I was playing Spades. I know, I know Spades at school.... Anyway, the guy I was playing with wasn't so good. We won the game, but afterwards everyone was saying how bad he was and how he didn't contribute to the win. I told him he did really good and he was a good partner. But... two seconds later, I leaned into my boyfriend and said "Oh my god, he sucks." I know that's really fake but what if I had told him to his face that he sucked? I would have lost a friend and hurt his feelings. I didn't want to be a mean girl. We did win so there was no need to get mad. Everyone has their fake moments. You can't be totally honest all the time.

When I walk down the hall I wonder are these the questions going through people's heads or am I just paranoid? Then again when others walk past me, I'm thinking the same thing. I mean I can actually go up to someone, tell them they look nice, but I'm really thinking: "What the hell is she wearing?" I mean, everyone does it no matter how young, old, rich, or poor. We all say what we are not really thinking.

What if people did actually say what they wanted to say? The world would be crazy. People would go off on bosses, teachers, friends, maybe even the President. Well, some people already do, but it would be so chaotic.

A good example would be my good friend who I've known for the last year. She's not afraid to say what she thinks if someone asks her, "Does this look nice?" And if she doesn't like it she has no problem saying, "I don't like it." I mean when she's talking to me I don't get offended because she's my best friend. But, wait a minute. She can't be the only one who says what she thinks. The only difference may be that she's totally honest to her friends.

People may actually shoot down others' confidence. They might think they are a good singer until someone comes around and says, "You suck." So, I wonder how many people's confidence have I shut down? Am I a mean person? Which goes back to my first question: how do people see me? If I get dressed and ask someone, "How do I look? Be honest." Before we answer this let's focus on the "honest" part.

To myself, I look nice. When I ask this question I want them to think the same. But what if they don't think so, what if they think I look horrible! So when I say "honest" I mean – and I think many people think – give me a good positive honest opinion. I think, how many people had to stop wearing their favorite jeans because someone was honest; how many people had to stop wearing that new shirt their parents bought them because someone was honest. I mean, being honest isn't bad if you know when to use it.

So, what about me? Am I a mean girl? I honestly can say that I haven't shut anyone down on purpose. I think I'm pretty good with drawing the line between being honest and being "too" honest. For me when it comes to being honest I want to come off as compromising. I want my judgment for them to be something they would expect. This way no one gets hurt. I want that person to feel she's happy because she sort of figured it out herself and I'm happy because she is. I know honesty is something people always search for in friends, family or a significant other. I mean being honest has its perks, but sometimes I wonder whether people can take the cut-throat truth?

The Pen Will Never Judge Me

What is life?
A solved puzzle that you get scrambled up to solve again?
Lots of mystery
Questions to be asked
and no matter how many answers I get
none seem to satisfy my taste for justification.
Justification for things that go wrong in life.

My inquisitiveness sometimes gets me into trouble,
Like the cat who wanders into the dog pen.
But after many times of being bitten
I still seek things,
still want to know what's beyond that wired fence.
I sometimes question questions that have been asked of me.

I refuse to give up on myself.
I plan to exceed all limits set up by society and myself.

Sometimes I can't see straight.
Life gets hazy and crazy but my pen brings such color.
I love to write.
I'm shy at times but the pen will not judge me.

I sometimes wonder where life is taking me.
Will I survive?
Does anyone ever achieve all of their goals?
Why do we feel pain?
Who said what pain was?
Who created pain?
Why are promises broken?
When will there be a breakthrough?

The ink will not lie to me, will not let me down.
The paper cannot hurt me.
I give my heart and soul to the notebook.
It is my escape plan, my legacy.
Through my writing I hope that those asleep will awaken.
Think thoughts, follow with actions, and be free.
Be themselves...like I can be me in ink
The shadows of my words stick to those who are consumed by them.
Taking them to another life, another day, like a dream.

Where Am I?

I'm in the zone, relaxed and quiet, a loud noise sounds off bringing chills down my spine and startling me. I walk through this dark room only to end up in a bright room that hurts my eyes. I'm looking at someone right across from me who's not very pleasing right now. As I come to my senses I realize I don't have a lot of time left. Look at the time; look at the time, why does it matter so much? Jump out of the warm liquid feeling cleansed and ready to dry. My attire is perfect. My scent is divine and now I'm ready. Where am I?

I sit and wait for a big bright vehicle. As it comes, I'm rushing to catch it with the wind blowing through my hair. The ride is very shaky as it jumps curbs and bounces on every ditch. I arrive at this familiar and sometimes pleasant place, seeing lots of people scrambling around like a fiesta of some kind. Where am I?

I walk down this long hallway checking out the scenery around me feeling relief as I get to my first destination. I start to walk, noticing many familiar faces and greeting them as if I just didn't see them less than twenty-four hours ago. Not knowing how the day is going to go I try to think to myself if I should be quiet, hyper or just go with the flow. Where am I?

Some people would probably say that I'm in my own little world dreaming, but I would say that I'm in another morning in my head. To me, this is just me viewing the day at another point of view.

Walking Concealers

I'm riding in the car, on the passenger side, and for no reason at all my eyes drift to the advisory sticker on the rearview mirror: "Objects in mirror are closer than they appear." I roll my eyes and click my tongue on the root of my mouth in total disgust. I'm thinking that this sticker somehow pertains to life. Yet what the hell does a sticker know? There are millions of people on this Earth crossing the path of mirrors, staring into a reflection completely distant from their true selves. These people are putting up fronts with staged personalities, trying to please the person next to them who unbeknownst to them is doing the exact same thing. We're all a bunch of walking concealers. Yes, we. I include myself. I guess until now, I've been in denial about my image. In my defense I can say that unlike most people, I don't know the person I'm trying to conceal. I've never met her.

As the ride continues, we pull into a gas station. The building is gray with rotted windows, rundown sides, and ancient pumps, possibly from years of neglect. I decide to stretch my legs, so I get out of the car and pace back and forth along the concrete. Just when I start to think that the scenery as a whole is depressing, I become mesmerized as I pass along a field of the most beautiful flowers I have ever set eyes on. The flowers are a reddish, pink color, and the mist on the tips of the petals glisten in the sunlight. The thick, green stems with leaves every now and then seem wax-like, almost too perfect. It almost makes me go from my, "the whole world against me" mood, to a seemingly cheeky persona.

But as I scan the field, this one immature flower grabs my attention. There seems to be a great amount of distance between it and the rest of the flowers, like it has its own soil patch. Something's wrong with it. Why out of all this beauty do I have to find something wrong? From the side, the petals are in an upright position, making the flower look completely closed. But at closer glance, I can see that the flower is on the verge of blooming like the others. It's partially opened at the top, almost like it was attempting to sprout, but it got stuck and couldn't. Maybe it got afraid...afraid that if it opened up, the world would reject it. It's thinking that the world would chew it up and spit it out, stripping it of all its security, leaving the flower in complete disarray. So it decides to play it safe, only semi-opening.

Safety does, however, have its consequences. Because the flower doesn't have a complete voice, the world can't hear it crying out those pain-filled tears of deep sorrow and regret. The world can't see it drowning in its own agonized pool of self-made depression, clinging to any and everything that gives it a temporary high. The world is completely oblivious to the flower's toxic state-of-being.

Why hasn't the flower given up on life already? Why hasn't it given up when it can only watch as its counterparts live a somewhat more satisfying life – a life more than its own – because it's truly not living. Life for the flower is merely a planning period – it plans to do this, it plans to do that, but in reality, planning is the only step the flower takes.

I make my way back to the Chevy, feeling no emotion one way or another. The world looks so big from here and when I think in terms of the flower, I wonder if something so small would even be missed if it was gone. I wonder if something so small even has some sort of significance in this world. If the flower were to die, say tomorrow, the world would keep spinning as if the flower hadn't been there in the first place. I wonder what the flower's gravestone would say, if it got one at all. Maybe something like: "Here lies the flower that didn't live at all."

We're off and away, in search of our destination. I take one last look at the mirror. I look past the wretched advisory sticker, past my so-called reflection, which I know is purely an illusion. I even look beyond the flower field background, which conceals all the fear. I take the mirror in as a whole.

25

I have nothing to say to you.
Nothing at all.

Seven years wearing a cute polka dot shirt
with a pink skirt and bows in my hair!
I'm looking at you wondering when you will realize
how much I care.

I follow behind, beggin' you to take me for ice cream.
All I want to be is up by my father
who I think is wonderful.

I grow up more and more thinking to myself
does my father love me.
Because you never come around.
You never call.

I can't believe
you don't even wanna'
say come and get me.
It's just the simple fact
that I think about how much
I'm a daddy's girl
and you don't even care.

I wonder everyday about our father
and daughter relationship.
I love you very much and
I really wish you would realize these things.

Dad, have you ever wondered
about if I was never here?
What would your life be like without a baby girl?
Your daughter (me).
I just wanted to see how you would feel or even think.

I have hard times sometimes
because I miss you in my life,
but you steady intend to be the same way all the time.

My feelings are always hurt
when it comes to you.
I can't always feel
this way about my father.
You only do so much for me because you say
you pay child support.
So what, it doesn't matter.
You should love to buy anything for me!
Why is it so hard for me to ask for $20?

I can't take this anymore.
My love for my father will always be there.
But when it comes down to the end do you really care?

Me.
Hello.
I'm a daddy's girl.

27

It's A Long Story

I know for sure that my Grammy is thinking about me, just as she did when she was alive. My Grammy was a beautiful and intelligent woman. Grammy and I had a strong bond. Because my mommie wasn't around for a long time, my Grammy and I developed a mother-daughter relationship. I loved everything about her.

My grandma's skin was like milk chocolate, not a bump in sight. She had soft cheeks, olive eyes and naturally-trimmed eyebrows. Her nose was perfect and plump, as if it were an apple ready to be picked. She had an openface gold tooth in the front of her mouth. Her lips were always dark as plums, lightly covered with gloss. I would make her kiss me over and over until her lipstick transferred from her lips to mine.

When she smiled at me, I felt as though I was the most loved person in the world. Her hair was like a long, long black silk curtain with bangs covering her eyes; it always smelled nice. She was thick and dressed nice even in her casual clothes. She wore jewelry every day that was gold and shiny; she had so much of it. My Grammy was a woman of wisdom. I told her she was the most beautiful woman in the world.

I called her everyday and I would rehearse my answers just because I knew she would ask me the same thing. Most of the time I would make up things to make it sound interesting. Most of the time I would say, "fine." I could imagine calling her right now.

GRANDMA: *Hey Denny. How was your day? What did you eat? How is everyone? What did you do in school today?"*

DENNY: *I don't know. Okay. Nothing Really.*

GRANDMA: *Your uncle told me about your talking back. I know you have things to say but you're a child and he's taking care of you. You're just like your mom, always having something to say. Sometimes it's best to keep your comments to yourself. You understand?*

DENNY: *Yes ma'am.*

GRANDMA: *Don't be sad, okay?*

DENNY: *Yes ma'am.*

When I called, she would ask the same questions.

GRANDMA: *Hey Denny. How was your day?*

DENNY: *Um, it was okay.*

GRANDMA: *Your uncle told me about your new job. I think it is good that you have it. It's a great way for you to learn how to be responsible. Do you like it so far?*

DENNY: *Yeah. Everyone is so nice and it's fun. It's like an extended family. I like it a lot. The only thing I didn't like is selling magazines. I hate them. My managers are always saying how we have to sell them, but I don't like them.*

GRANDMA: *Yeah, Denny, but that's your job and if they're paying you to do something then you should do it and if you don't feel it's right for you then you can find a new job. You know?*

DENNY: *Yes, ma'am.*

GRANDMA: *So tell me about school? How have your grades been?*

DENNY: *It seems like they are okay for the most part but they went down. I think it's because I can't manage my time.*

GRANDMA: *Now you know what you need to do about that. Why are you so busy?*

DENNY: *I think it's because of my job.*

GRANDMA: *Well you should either learn how to manage your time or quit your job.*

DENNY: *I'm trying. I really don't want to quit. The only class I'm not doing well in is Algebra II.*

GRANDMA: *Well, maybe I could call Chell and have her help you. Is anyone helping?*

DENNY: *Yes, ma'am.*

The memory of her voice is so strong, it reminds me of a conversation we had before, out of all the conversations we had, this one sticks in my brain the most. I picked up the phone, dialed her number and waited for the phone to ring. She picked up.

GRANDMA: *Hello?*

DENNY: *Hey Grammy.*

GRANDMA: *Hey Denny. How was your day?*

DENNY: *It was okay. We just finished eating dinner.*

GRANDMA: *What did you eat?*

DENNY: *Some rice, broccoli and some meat. Banana pudding too.*

GRANDMA: *What meat did you eat?*

DENNY: *I don't know. I think it was brown or something.*

GRANDMA: *You don't know what different kinds of meats there are?*

DENNY: *No ma'am.*

GRANDMA: *Which ones do you know?*

DENNY: *Chicken and fish.*

GRANDMA: *Well, Denny, I don't think that's good. Maybe you should learn your meats or stop eating them, okay?*

DENNY: *Yes, ma'am.*

That was my last phone conversation with Grammy. She passed from cirrhosis of the liver. I remember our conversation. After we talked I decided that I would only eat the meats I knew because my Grammy told me to. To this day, I only eat fish and chicken. When people ask me why, I smile and say, "It's a long story." Now that I'm older, I realize that my Grammy didn't really want me to stop eating meats, but I took everything she said to heart.

MIKE JONES

Granny

Felt I was left in dis world once my granny was gone
March 4, 2005 when she left me alone.
Tried to keep it gangsta in my eyes instead da tears fell
Sittin back in da corner reminiscing her smell,
Thinking why did she have to go and leave me like this?
Didn't even have a chance to give her one last kiss.
Remembering how she used to come and light up da room,
Yeah, wit dat smile about as bright as da moon.
Hopin' one day maybe I could see her again,
Go on Saturday runs like we did on da weekends.
Wishing at least she could've even seen me grow up,
Or at least she could've seen da cap and gown I threw up
Still gon get on my grind and always make her feel proud
While I'm on dis rollercoaster of life making my heart pound.
I'm gon protect and serve da family like da LAPD.
Always have you in my heart granny, R.I.P.

31

What If?

My mama had six miscarriages before she had me and I was the only one who didn't die. Right before I was born my mama had a child name Jamie. Jamie suffered from Trisomy 13TH syndrome. Instead of her having the normal X and Y, her 13TH chromosome was XXY. She had a cleft lip and an opening in the top palate of her mouth. She never made it home from the hospital. She died ten months after her birth in the same place. After her death, my mother changed her own name to Jamie after her daughter. My mother considered me her miracle. She says if it weren't for me she would have nothing. I feel without her I would be nothing.

When my mama was pregnant with me, she got really sick. She had no appetite and her skin was turning very pale. She was losing more and more energy every day. She went to the hospital, but the doctor could not figure out what was wrong. She didn't know she was pregnant at the time. She was just stressed out. She died and the doctors revived her. She told me she could hear my grandmother screaming in the background, but she couldn't say anything. She also said that she could hear God talking to her. He told her to blink twice for "yes" and once for "no." He would ask her questions. He asked her if she knew he was. She blinked twice. He asked if she really wanted to leave her mother hurt like this. She blinked once. Right then she opened her eyes. My grandmother burst out in tears again. That's when my mama found out she was pregnant with me and was diagnosed with diabetes.

She's been both parents to me, and she is what has made me as strong as I am today. She looks exactly like me; well, I look exactly like her. She is a very loving, caring person with a kind heart, just like her mother (my grandma). My mama and grandma both support me in everything I do. They have my back no matter what, whether I'm right or wrong. If I go to jail, they're going with me. They are the best parents I could have. Like my mother paid $337.00 dollars for my class ring and my grandma paid $365.00 so I could go on a college road show.

I remember a day that we had at school where our parents could come and explain their careers. I'll never forget this day. My mother was the only parent to show up. She really impressed the class and made me so proud. And, I remember all the musicals and concerts that she sat through in elementary school. All the basketball games she attended, all the birthday parties. Every year was special. One year I had a horse and pony, one year a party with a clown, Chucky Cheese's, two hotel parties, a family fun center, skating rink parties and many more.

I can't imagine life without her. Once, when I was eight years old, as I lay on the couch in not much of a deep sleep, I heard a whisper, "Misha, Misha," but I ignored it. I continued on dreaming and again I could hear this gentle voice, "Misha, Misha." So, I opened my eyes, and what I woke up to was the worst thing a child could experience. I saw my mother on the love chair sweating and shaking and having a hard time moving or projecting a sound. I didn't know what to do, she could hardly speak. Then I asked, "Mama, what's wrong?" She said, "Sugar. I need sugar," as if it killed her to say these words. So I ran into the kitchen and grabbed a cupful of sugar, running nonstop wasting sugar all through the house from the kitchen to the living room I finally made it. I dumped the sugar all into her mouth and within twenty seconds her sugar was back up and she was functioning properly. This had been the biggest scare I ever had in my life. My mother then explained her condition to me. She was a diabetic and she had to control her sugar or it could be life threatening. From that day on I have paid close attention to my mother and her eating habits. I couldn't imagine what I would do if something happened to her. Just think if I hadn't been lazy and went upstairs and gotten into my bed. My mother would have died.

She often tells me that she doesn't know where she would be or what she would be if weren't for me, but I don't consider myself her miracle. I consider her my blessing, because God could not assign me to a better mother. I appreciate her so much. She means the world to me. She keeps the glow in my eyes. We were meant to guide each other through life and there couldn't be a better couple.

33

The Curse

I think my family is cursed! I know someone is probably thinking I'm crazy for saying such a thing. I'm not too fond of witches and voodoo dolls. Also, I don't believe in witchcraft or anything, so I've come to the conclusion that my family is cursed.

See, we have a vast and drastic amount of deaths in our family. Someone is always dying. The worst part is that, as my grandmother always says, "Bad things come in threes." And she's right. Because if someone dies in January, then somebody else dies and it always comes in threes. And all of these deaths have made me superstitious.

Old people say that when you see those little black birds on your lawn, then that's a sign that death is near. And I used to always see all those black birds on our lawn and I thought death was coming. I just figured that someone was about to die. And usually someone does die – if not in my family, then someone in the world.

My great-grandmother has sixteen children. It is sad to say that there are only five of them left. I have a very big family. In my family we have five generations. Many people say, "Wow! That is amazing to have so many great-great-great aunts." But for me, with all the death in my family, it is a blessing. Although another problem in my family is that a lot of them don't get along. So when we have family reunions, there is so much hostility that everyone doesn't even show up. Then I say to myself: "Why is my family so difficult? Why do we go through so many problems? How did we get this curse and how do I break it?"

With all the death and the problems, I have certain people (and pets) in my life who make me feel blessed. In life there are many things I want to accomplish. I have extraordinary dreams and desires that I hope to fulfill. In fact, there are several inspiring people in my life who support my dreams.

I am fortunate to have my sister. My big sister is my main inspiration. She is one of the biggest role models in my life right now. She encourages me to do whatever I want in life. She pushes me to acknowledge college, occupations, and other opportunities. She doesn't like pinning ribbons on me a lot because when she was my age she went through things that she doesn't want me to go through now. Like, she became a teenage mother and she doesn't want me to make the mistakes she made.

My sister pushes me because she wants me to stay on the right track. She looks at me like I'm her daughter, but we still have like a sisterly bond. When she got married, I was the junior bridesmaid and she was the bride. She wore her veil and she bought me a veil to wear too. The photographer captured us together, my sister fixing the veil on my head. The pictures were beautiful.

My grandmother picks me up when I fall; it's like placing a bandage over my wound. Her words give me encouragement to stay strong and go on and on. I mean she is an amazing woman who's loved by many. She has these big bold bountiful eyes and she wears a flowery apron in the kitchen. Then there are these big squarish glasses that she puts on to read. When she speaks it is like old sayings and hymn songs. My grandmother is an old wise person when I need advice.

My grandma calls me pastry. Although she spends most of her time in the kitchen, I sometimes find her in the living room with a grande cup of coffee. She loves it black with two tablespoons of cream and two tablespoons of sugar. My grandmother is always trying to get people to eat something. Especially cornbread. That's the best. And greens.

She sits around eating peppermints all day. She loves to clean. She hates wrinkles in the bed or crumbs on the floor. She's just so loving. She has a way about her so that you know what you should do. She has this smile of gold that lights the room and she is an amazing woman.

And then there's my dog. I have this unique dog that's quite special, more than any other dog I know. His name is Jigga. He's special in so many ways. Jigga's special because he's a shitzu and weighs more than any other toy dog I know. He is special because he eats gourmet dog food at the price of ninety-seven cents a container and that still doesn't satisfy his hunger. The head of my household, my sister, doesn't buy one container, she buys a whole box.

Did I mention Jigga's very greedy and he sure knows how to beg? He sits up under the kitchen table with his big, bold eyes and his long tiny tongue waiting for me to drop a piece of chicken or two. Oh yeah, I forgot to mention that he knows how to sit, jump, and shake my hand with his paw. Well that's only if you're offering him a piece of garlic bologna.

Jigga is really smart too. When he is thirsty, he takes his paw and pushes his bowl toward the sink. He doesn't like to be in a room alone either. He's so human. He likes ice and he'll lie on his back. He's just a unique dog.

In spite of all the confusion and chaos in my family, I have a friend who's an only child and she told me one day that she was jealous of my life because I have all these people who were special to share it with. I couldn't understand why she would feel this way. She had everything, while I on the other hand was less fortunate than her, but I seem to be much happier. Me I'm fine, I'm ok. I guess having a cursed family isn't bad after all. What more can I ask for!

From the Bottom to the Top

Nothing – No money, no friends, no family, no food, no home. This is what fail-ing is to me. Failure is what I am most afraid of in life, period. When you see people on the corner begging, they have failed. Failing to me means you are at the bottom. When you are at the bottom people look down on you. I don't want to fail.

Ol' Dude is a dude in my hood that I see like every day. Ol' dude is like 5' 11" and skinny like a pencil, with a caramel complexion. He has the stench of a dumpster with old food in it on a hot summer day in St. Louis. His face is skinny with big dark eyes. It makes him look like an owl in the night. His hair is nappy and sharp like a head full of blades. He looks scary and is always watching his back as if someone is about to do something to him. He looks just shameful.

When I step into a crib, I see success, a proud man who stands tall like the Statue of Liberty. Head high, face clean and glossy as a freshly waxed hard wood floor. Everything about this man says that he is successful, his swag is proud, as if he were some kind of king. This man is my daddy. Sometimes when I am alone in my thoughts I think, who will I be? Will I be Ol' Dude or will I be my daddy? When I am down I feel like Ol' Dude, when I am up I feel like my dad. I wonder sometimes, do your thoughts have an effect on who you become? Like if you think positive, then you become successful but if you think negative, you become a failure.

Success to me is having more than enough money to give my family everything they need and want. I want to retire early and never have to work my whole life. I want people to say that Ken Clark is the most successful person they know. I wanna' live in Cali, on the beach, in a house almost as big as the White House. I want to work in an office and on the outside of the building I want to have the name of my big sport agency. I wanna' go home to my wife and kids and be living happy as a kid on Christmas morning. Success is the cure to my fear of failing. The more successful I am, the happier I will be.

BRIANA PEPPERS

Clayton Corners

All through life you have to change. But what kind of change is too much? Sure, I had been to classes on conduct in the work world. But conduct in the real work world was nothing like the bullet points in the textbooks they give you. No one told me I would have to bust out of a shell that a group of strangers had already put me in. No one let me know the gossip and politics of the work world. I felt alone.

I used the Saint Louis Internship Program as my first dose of professional training. They taught us things like which fork to use, how to write a resume, and how to operate copy machines and fax machines. Basically the program prepared me to step in the corporate world. That lasted March through May, every Saturday, training from 8:00 AM – 1:00 PM There were about 200 students. At the end of the program the students chose their top three desired internship sites. My first choice was the Mayor's Office. My second choice was a law firm and my final choice was a site dealing with science. Some people got assigned to police stations, the Marriott, art galleries and businesses. I was looking forward to the Mayor's office, but I got a law firm. I was disappointed at first, but I was okay because I got a site and least it was a law firm.

My first taste of corporate life was at the tender age of fifteen. Sure I was nervous the first day, but by the third day, I was tired of going. But look at the situation. Here it is the beginning of the summer, 6:00 A.M., and I'm on my way to work. Work! I was held captive until 4:30 PM I used to dread going into the building, especially in the elevator on the way up. I mean, everyone else is sleeping and here it is July and I'm going to work. Everyday I would arrive at work at 7:30 and leave at 4:30. My mom would drop me off, and then sometimes I would catch the bus home. The best thing about the job was going to lunch with my friend, who I'd known since sixth grade. I looked forward to those lunches and going home.

The hours would pass so slowly because there really wasn't anything for me to do. I didn't even have a place to be. When I first got there, I used the file room as a place to set my things and have a seat. But toward the end of the summer, I had no place to be, so I would sit on a stool.

It took me practically the entire summer to understand the "ways" of the work world. I didn't understand why all of the secretaries were women and all of the attorneys were men. I was puzzled by a meeting with nothing but Caucasian males in the main meeting room. I can still remember walking past the grand room with a long marble top table and twenty-four chairs. I was absolutely stunned. I don't remember if I was shocked because of the meeting or shocked because I actually realized what so many others had already told me before. I called my Mom at lunch and I told her there was not one woman, much less an African American. African Americans. There was a total of four including myself. One man, two women, and me. Naive, frustrated, misjudged me.

I felt all alone. My co-workers automatically assumed the farthest I had been in the world was Ferguson. They assumed my mother and father did not work, or were even together. I suppose they figured my parents didn't even know where I was. But they did, and I have been farther than Ferguson, Missouri.

So why the prejudgment? I remember my co-worker asked me, "How do you afford to wear the things you wear?" I wish I could have responded honestly and instead I didn't. Instead, I just smiled and gave a general, half-thought-out answer. That was one of my true wake-up calls. When she asked me that question, it confirmed everything I'd been thinking. There's a whole person standing here, why think something like that? What answer did she expect me to say?

I stayed at the law firm the entire duration of the internship. In two months I learned how some professionals behave. The next step is just accepting how they are. I do not regret my internship. It was truly a rewarding experience. I watched and I learned. It's all a game and that is fine. I didn't know it going in, but now I am absolutely positive of it.

Now I am officially ready to play. I know the rules and I am ready to win. If you calculate your opponent's moves you can plan your moves. Checkers, dominoes, careers. In order to play your game and win you have to first play their game. Change is not a bad thing. In some cases it is for the best. The object of the game is just to know when change is too much.

Conversation in Black and White

People call me racist.

Who?

Just people. But I don't think I'm racist, I think I just ask the questions that everybody else is afraid to ask.

What questions?

Well... My teacher in class. He's white. We were talking about those people who bought a camera at Best Buy and when they got it home, they found a jar of spaghetti sauce?

I don't know that story.

So I asked whether the people got their money back and the girl who was telling the story replied, "No," and so I assumed the people were black, but I asked the girl about the couple's race and she said they were white, and I said the couple should've got their money back because of their race.

Why would white people get their money back and not the black couple?

I don't think they should've gotten their money back. They just would.

But why?

Because everybody would think the black people stole the camera.

Oh.

And so my white teacher called me racist and my class was full of black kids and they were surprised that I said that, but I know they were thinking the same thing.

So do you think you're racist?

When they call me that, I think they think I hate other races, so I don't call myself that. I think I just say what others are thinking and in some cases, the truth. I think I stereotype races, but I don't think that's racism.

———————

Okay. I have a question for you. What's the definition of racism?

I don't know. It's like when one race thinks they're better than the other.

39

Right. Here's a definition from the dictionary.
The belief that some races are inherently superior (physically, intellectually, or culturally) to others and, therefore, have a right to dominate them.
Is that you? Is that what you believe?
No.
So why do you think people call you a racist?
I think racism is when you don't like them.
Is stereotyping a form of racism?
I don't think stereotypes are so bad, or talking about them because they came from somewhere. People aren't just making it up, and they help you see where people are coming from. You can't do anything about it.
About what?
Stereotypes. People are probably really like that, so you can't change them. You can just try to understand.
What do you think the stereotypes are?
A sixteen-year old African American girl's gonna' get pregnant. But I don't think black girls have it as bad as black boys because everyone thinks they're gonna' drop out and sell drugs. Ain't as easy as they think.
Why?
Everybody doesn't have money and all they can do is try to get money.
Sounds unfair.
That's all they see and all they know is just what they see.
Who?
White people.
But don't you think that conversation, at least talking like we're doing helps?
Helps what?
Helps break down the stereotypes.
I don't think the stereotypes can be broken.
Are the stereotypes true of you?
No, it's not true.
Why?
Probably not. Cuz' that's just not what I want. People already think that's gonna' happen to you, so you make sure that's not going to happen.
So what do you want to do that's different?
I wanna' be on Oprah. Anything to be on Oprah. I'll be a financial expert on Oprah.

———————————

My sister sent me an e-mail and it had a whole lot of questions and you had to erase their answers and put in yours. One of the questions was what are you most afraid of and she said, "God." So I erased God and I put in that I'm afraid to be just another black person and I wondered if that was racist.
What do you mean?

I don't know. Like racist, especially since I'm black.
   Why is that bad?
People look at us like we're "nothing." I don't know.
   Yeah, you do.
They just look down on us. We're black and we're poor.
   *But there are African-American people who are not poor and people don't look
   down on them, like Barack Obama.*
He's rich and lucky.

———————

   Are there any obstacles that you can't overcome?
I don't know. Sometimes I feel like giving up. It doesn't matter if you are a lawyer
or a teller or a worker a McDonald's, people are still going to look down on you.
And if you get authority or a superior position, people are going to wonder how
and why you got where you are.

———————

I don't meet that many white people.
My friend said if she's around white people she would act the same. I don't
agree. Every time a black person is around a white person they try to talk proper
or not how they usually talk. They don't do things they would usually do. I think
the only way they would act normal is if they are comfortable around them or
know them really well.

———————

We went to a College Fair and there were like five black parents and like a hun-
dred white parents. And even if they were black, they were like black people
acting white.
   Why weren't there more black people?
'Cuz black people don't care.
   Do you think they don't care or is it a problem with money?
Probably. I mean why should they care if they don't have money? Why should
they go to college knowing they can't pay for it?
   Wouldn't they have more of a reason to go to college?
Not if you don't have money to pay.
   What about scholarships and financial aid?
I mean, that's an option. They probably don't think about that.
   Do you want to go to college?
Yep, but sometimes I think that I'm not.
   Why?
'Cuz it's still not going make you happy. Sometimes it doesn't matter to me. I
don't want to be caring about it.
   Because it's too hard.

41

Yeah. It's not gonna' change anything for real.

What would you change?

Once you graduate from college, people are still going look at you the same way.

How's that?

Just black. You're still goin' be nothing.

Do you have any African-American role models – people you respect?

Oprah.

———————

They're not going to acknowledge you for who you are. They're not going to congratulate you; they're going to wonder how you got there and how they're gonna' take it from you.

What about Oprah?

It's true for Oprah when she started out. They're used to her now.

So your answer is to just give up? Because what's the use?

Accept what you got. Be thankful for what you got. Don't stress. Just be happy with your family and that's something. That's better than college, anyway. Cuz it's not gonna' change anything.

It sounds to me like you given into the stereotypes that you want to reject.

You might try to go to college, but you're gonna' realize that there's no point in going because you're still black.

So what's the alternative for you? What would you do instead?

Don't let yourself be stressed out; just don't worry about money.

I see what you're thinking, where you're coming from. Not everybody has to go to college. There's something to be said for self-acceptance, but it bothers me when you say that you think somehow you're inferior because you are black, that you will always be inferior and that there is no way that will ever change, whether you go to college or not.

The people that are going to be happy that you got somewhere are the other black people.

So what about you? Outside of college, outside of the future, what about you? It bothers me that you think you are somehow not enough, so why try? Right here and right now, I hear you saying that I'm black, I'm inferior, and that's never going to change. It sounds so unfair, like you've given up on yourself before you even give yourself a chance. You are buying into the stereotypes that you say aren't so bad, but I got to tell you, I think they're really, really bad if they have made you feel that way.

I don't know what to say. It is bad, but sometimes it's the truth and I don't think it's ever gonna' change. It's 2007 and I don't think it's ever going to change. That's how I feel and a lot of other people too.

Well, I have to tell you that I think you're wrong about the stereotypes. I think they're really wrong. And, I think you have already broken the mold.

Sometimes, I think what I am saying is not really the way I feel – all the time; it's the way the majority feels.

So, we come around to you again. YOU! The celebration of Brianna. Where we started our conversation. You, Brianna, asking the questions that no one else wants to ask. Taking risks. You are speaking for yourself, but you say you are also speaking up for the majority – for those who are afraid to speak?

Not afraid, they're probably not afraid, they just don't say it.

Kinda' like the jar of spaghetti sauce, right?

Right.

TANNER SENTER

Provin' People Wrong

Is the United States government ever going to have some change? Will there ever be someone besides a middle-aged white man in the oval office? Will there ever be a female or an African American running this country? Will the citizens ever accept an African American President when they are so used to their traditional ways?

Well, the citizens will eventually have to. Changes are coming every day, and more and more African Americans and women are holding higher and higher government offices. It's time for new ideas to come from perspectives of different races and genders. Who better for the job than...Me!! – An African American Male?

Many may say this will never happen. Especially for a black man. But when I start my campaign the American people will be ready to accept me. My visions and ideas are strictly for the greater good. There's no secret agenda in my ideas – like previous (or current) Presidents.

The bad ideas of many leaders have directly affected me. My mother is paying taxes that don't do anything for her or for any other American citizens. The Government spent $20 billion in 2001 and is expected to spend $200 billion in 2007 on war. My goal is to clean the house of our citizens before moving to our neighbors. The lives of my family members and friends are being risked to protect the lives of Iraqi citizens, rather than their own friends and family.

As a young black male it's already hard to accomplish much since most people judge a book by its cover. Since I dress comfortably – baggy clothes, big coat – people see the thuggish side, but not the intelligent side of me. People look down on black males. It's not only other races, but even black people looking down on each other.

A good example was when my brother and I went to a store that was run by Arabian people to buy some gum. They made us feel uncomfortable with their muggin' eyes just watching us. When we went to check out we put the gum on the counter and they just looked at us. No movement. No words. We literally had to put the gum in their face before we were acknowledged. This was a big problem that I have taken the liberty to solve by my example and my ideas.

In the future, I'll be out there bringing my ideas to the people of this country. My slogan: "There's always a first time." So the next time you see a young African American male running down the street with a big coat, don't assume that he's in trouble or causing trouble because he could be your future president. Look out for me.

Just Keep Goin'

The question in the air is who inspires me? Everyone in the world has an issue, so when I see people smiling, it lets me know that I am not the only person going through things. You never know what people are going through at home, work, or school, so when people smile, it makes me happy. If you were to come to my school, you would notice so much stuff going on, it might make you want to break down.

This is what you need to know. There's fighting over boys. There's back-stabbing. There's gossip. Say this person gets together with someone else, they just gotta' tell someone. Say your friend gets together with another one of your friends and then they tell you. You just gotta' tell someone else. There's gossip about sex and other stuff – like who talks to who, who goes with who. Then a fight starts. Every day. It's mainly girls, fighting over boys. But if I see someone happy and I know they have it bad – like people talking about them – that inspires me to know that I should appreciate what I have.

Most kids at school don't have all the things I have. I have a mother and a father. I live with my mother, and my father is in my life. Most kids don't have that. My mother takes care of me, and I don't want or need for anything. I have friends, and most people don't have that. People go home and might want to kill themselves because so much stuff is going on at school – like they were bullied or had some things going on, but when you see them you would never know.

I have people in my life that I can depend on or lean on to help me deal with everything. My mother is one because she handles a lot too. My mother is a person who smiles underneath it all. She's always happy, and I know that she has bills to pay and sometimes she doesn't have the money. She inspires me to work harder in school and, more importantly, to work hard in life. She always tells me to go to school, get good grades, and don't be a dropout. Every day she pushes me harder and harder. Whether she's putting me on punish-ment or cursing me out, it all helps me do better. She's been through a lot, but she's strong.

My cousin is another person who inspires me. She is a single parent with two children. She tries her best to provide for her kids, and to give them all they want and need. She is twenty – five years old, and she helps me when I need someone to talk to about anything. Her advice is good and it's good to talk to her because she is not that much older than me. She's strong. Even when she is going through anything, she always makes sure that she looks good. One day she can fight with her baby's father, but guaranteed, the next day she will look like nothing happened. If you didn't know her, you wouldn't know that anything is wrong with her. She lets me know that things will be okay.

You look at me and you think you see somebody who is comfortable with herself, but I've been through a lot. And I don't want to tell you about it because then I'll start crying. I just stay to myself. I have friends, but I don't always trust them. I have people I lean on and I know they will help me deal with what I go through. When I walk in school or when something is wrong with my life, I keep on smiling.

I'm Just Being Me

I work at Kentucky Fried Chicken – that's a fast food restaurant. Smiling is a key thing to them. One day we had an inspector visiting us. Before she came the managers were like, "Make sure you smile." I was like, "Why all of a sudden you all want us to do all this smiling when on a daily basis the boss don't smile and we don't either?"

It was just awkward to try to make us do something to impress people because that's not what we really do. If we did smile every day, then we would be used to doing it when she came. So when the woman got there she was observing, and I smiled when there was something to smile for. I wasn't just walking around smiling for nothing. When the woman was evaluating us she said we needed to smile more. She wasn't really talking to me then, she was talking to another boy. He just smiled and started doing something else.

The boss made a big thing out of us smiling, so I was like, "When do you all want us to smile?" She was like, "You should smile all the time when the customers are here." They printed up signs and posted them everywhere saying everyone should "wear a smile at all times." I don't pay attention to that because there is no need to walk around fake smiling.

Smiling is good in its place, but when you fake smile those are the worst ones because everyone can see the fakeness through it. I'll smile at the customers, but not when it's fake. I'm not just going to stand there with a frown on my face. I greet the customers. I don't really need someone else to tell me to do that.

When people tell me to smile, that really frustrates me. If I'm not smiling, there is nothing to smile for. People say I look mean when I don't smile. To tell the truth, I totally disagree. I look like me whether I'm smiling or not. Just because people tell me to smile doesn't mean I'm gonna smile. Actually that makes me angry so that I don't even want to smile. Maybe it's me.

I wonder, why do people put on these fronts? I know for a fact that people don't walk around always smiling just because. I will smile when necessary, but as far as walking around cheezing all the time that's not me. I'm not a fake. And me just acting so joyous and smiling for no reason would be fake. I'm being real and most of all, I'm being me.

Almost Doesn't Count

Closeness. Man, that's a strong word. To me closeness is being together with someone or trying to build a future with someone. I don't have any problems getting friends or calling my friends "my close friends." Man, this is hard to admit: I have never had a boyfriend, but I don't think I need one.

My brother always tells me that I do need a boyfriend because I have never had one. I see my friends that have boyfriends and I am by myself. I am responsible, kind, respectful, honest, strong-minded, and a very outgoing young lady. I don't know what's the matter. Am I just the type to be friends? Closeness is not a problem for me at all. Everyday I wish I could have a boyfriend that's not friend material, meaning, he is a friend, but thinks of me as more than a friend.

During my first year in high school, I hung out with upperclassmen. I met a boy who I'll call "J." He was smart, funny, and responsible, all the things you look for. So the school year went by and we started talking as friends, but as we talked, I started liking him more than a friend and he liked me. We hung out together and we enjoyed each other's company. One day he asked me to be his girlfriend. I got so excited. I was happy. But, I hesitated and wondered if he was serious. So I told him that I would think about it. He called that same night asking me if I thought about it. I told him that I would have the answer the next day. When we got to school, I started thinking about if I got close to him would he break my heart? Would he do something to me that would not let me get close to anyone?

The next day I had a field trip. I came back to school excited to tell him my answer: "yes." When I found him, he was talking to one of my friends. I got so mad that I went over and started yelling and cursing at him, and at my supposed-to-be friend.

He told me that they were just talking. I said, "Her up all under you is NOT talking." He couldn't really say anything. I left the room in anger. He ran out of the room to find me and he said, "I really like you and I don't want to talk to her. I want to talk to you." I told him that I felt something different between us besides being friends. I also told him that I had seen him talking to my friends so many times before, but he denied it. So I told him that maybe we should stop talking for a lil' bit. He kept asking why and I told him that I felt like I was getting close to him.

When my second year of high school started, I still felt something between me and him. We started talking as friends again, but I knew that there was a boundary, a limit on how close I could get to him without getting hurt. He asked me to be his girlfriend again. All I could say was that I didn't know, that we would have to see. It was his last year in high school, so I had to make a decision. Did I want to be with a person that I really liked for the first time in my life or did I want to be with him just because he was leaving?

In the end, we didn't become boyfriend and girlfriend. He was the first person that I grew close to. He was the first person who made me define what "closeness" is. As much as I might dream about having a boyfriend in my life, I think for now, I'm not ready. I'm not ready because I'm trying to figure out me first. Me First!

The Answer Girl

I'm the girl that knows the answers without any thought to the question.
The answer pops into my head and it just comes out.
I don't raise my hand because there is no time for it.
The thought is there and it's out of my mouth in an instant.
For being such an "at the moment" answer girl,
I can't answer a question directly asked to me.
The teacher will address me and all thoughts flee,
nothing comes to mind.
However, when the question is thrown out there
and asked to the class in general...
then I know the answer.
When I blurt it out some kids get angry
because it has only been a second since the teacher asked.
The other students yell at me for not letting them have a chance to answer
AND for not raising my hand.
If I were to stop to raise my hand
the answer would come...
and go.
The teacher would address my raised hand and I would try to answer but alas
the thought would flee.
When I answer these questions it is in any class.
One's I hate and one's I like.
People ask if I know all the answers because I like the subject,
But that's not the case.
I just know the answers.

A Child of "How?"

I wasn't a child of why.
I was a "how does that work?" girl.
How do the clock hands turn?
How do VCRs work?
When I'm curious as to how something works, I take it apart.
I take apart CD players to see how they read the CD.
I've taken apart telephones to see how the wires relate.
Curiosity gets the better of me and it's not always for the best.
I'll take something apart and end up breaking it.
Then I can no longer "process" it.
I'm a ROI.
Random Object Investigator.

Self-Portrait

Freckles of my father,
Skin from the golden sun.
Nose of my mother,
Lips the color of bubble gum.
Eyes cocoa-brown like the earth in the summer,
A mind of wisdom prevents a blunder.
Hair wild and untamable like a jungle lion,
My locks curl, twirl, and whirl, there's no hidden.
Hair on my arms black in the shadows, golden in the light,
Limbs of my body, all-full of might.
My hands mold clay,
My feet walk astray.
Skin filled with white leopard spots,
In winter, goose bumps rise to the mountaintops.
Being 5'10'' with a body hard to hide,
I'm not afraid to show what's deep down inside.
Personality striking, like a bolt of lightning, or a reality check,
My brutal honesty of the world might be your best bet.

I've been asked many times, over and over again, "Why do you feel the way you do?" This would be a quick and simple question to answer for the average person, but I'm much more complex. At times, I just give the person a bad look, I ignore them at other times, or I look them in the eye and say, "because" to give the impression that my reasons are much too broad to go into detail. There are people who don't even bother to ask because after getting to know me, they can sense I'm mean, bold, and strongly opinionated.

I know that some people wonder why anybody would want, and sometimes even enjoy, being mean. There are those who would say, in a little stuck up voice, "Well clearly, she lacks self-confidence and copes with it by picking on others." That might be the case for most "bullies" like psychologists think. They

53

think they know, and they have no idea. I say those who question me haven't been oppressed by reality as many times as I have.

"Being held back and kicked down by life over and over again" is a statement not a lot of people make because they don't view their life as being that bad, and those who do say it sometimes don't realize how good they have it. Normally, I would give examples to prove myself right, but I'm not ready to reveal my secretive past, to anyone. But I will say that one of the things that contributed to my outcast personality is being multiracial. It's not that I am at a disadvantage automatically for being black, white, and Indian, but there are people who would never accept me because I was "too white to be actin' black," as if the role of being black is a part in a play, or I was "too ghetto to be white."

Another social bridle is that I am naturally shy when I don't really know the people I'm around. As a little kid, I was extremely shy. Boys would pick on me because at the time, I was much smaller than them. To this day, I have flashbacks of them taunting me, irking my soul, making me want to explode with rage.

I also remember my cousin, who is also a boy. He would torture me when his parents (my aunt and uncle) weren't around. Because he was a lonely and extremely overweight idiot, he used to lock me in the bathroom by tying a cord to the door knob and attaching the other end to my room across the hall. If I was in my room, he would do the exact same thing and I would be stuck in my room. He locked me in the basement because the lock was on his side, and he would be upstairs in my room messing with my stuff. He locked me out of the kitchen and I would starve until he got bored and let me in. There was tons more. When I got fed up and did the little kid thing and told, my aunt and uncle wouldn't believe me! They'd say "Nuh uhh... He ain't do that." As I grew older, males became the target for my hatred. This is why I pick on them now.

The past hasn't only made me mean; it's taught me hard lessons to learn that some people spend their whole life repeating because it takes them more than one time to learn from experience. Those who know me just think I'm mean for no reason, but I always have a reason for anything I do.

54

I Hate Morning Time

The title says it all. I really do hate mornings, and anyone who told you otherwise is lying. I hate how the sun slowly rises at 6 AM like a retarded game of peek-a-boo. If my life were a cartoon, I would be the evil villain who tried to take away the sun forever. Forget about plants dying, chaos, and another ice age (it was coming eventually), I WANT IT GONE! I was born at 5:01 PM, so naturally, I'm nocturnal. From the time I wake up (6 AM) for school until 3 PM, I'm a zombie. I'm conscious and aware of what's going on, but sometimes, I feel like I'm having an out of body experience.

When I'm worn out and tired from a long day at school, boring hours of yearbook staff, and brutal back-aching hours at work, I get home (about 10 or 11), and I have the strangest urge to stay up, as if I just woke up from a long nap, charged with energy. Maybe I was a vampire in a past life?

I also hate overly sweet breakfast food in the morning. I don't wanna eat crap that's sweeter than candy, like syrup and icing on cinnamon buns, right after I wake up. It makes me sick, and milk is the only thing that keeps me from puking up syrup and waffles.

And in the summer time, who the hell gave my neighbors the right to mow their half dead lawn at 9 in the morning. You know, it's called a summer vacation for a reason, and I'd like to take advantage of it for as long as I can. And then they have the nerve to get mad because I'm up at 11 PM playin' my music.

It's called payback.

ME

I could say that I am the typical teenager, but I'm not. I do typical teenage stuff like eat, sleep, talk on the phone, go to parties, sleep, hang out with friends and sleep some more. Oh, and let's not forget the issues with my parents, working, after school activities, and the most important one of all, the good times with my friends and my boyfriend. I bet you're thinking, what makes you so different from other teenagers then? Well, what makes me different is that I'm me; it's just that plain and simple.

About Me

Let's see, what do I want you to know about me? My name is Jasmine, but everyone calls me JJ. I am a 17 year-old student. I'm about 5'5" with brown skin, shoulder length hair with sandy brown highlights (or cookies and cream as the L'Oreal highlight kit would say). I'm 116 pounds, slim/athletic/model physique. I always keep my hair and nails done and love to accessorize. I'm a little conceited, but hey, who isn't nowadays? Many people think that since I'm a model, I can't run track. They think it's impossible because it's like oil and water, they don't mix. But... at 2:45 you can find me in the weight room with my hair in a ponytail with sweats on lifting weights. Both hobbies keep me busy, but I am still able to maintain good grades, no weight, and excellent grades.

The Family Scene

I'm not going to pretend like I have the best family in the world, because I don't. I have my problems with them and I'm pretty sure that they have their problems with me. My parents would probably say that it's my attitude, but they don't have the best attitudes either. My mom is cool. It could be her loving children that keep her youthful. My mom likes to go shopping, listen to my music, she loves to talk, and she doesn't have a problem with me going out with friends. She really shows her age when she says stuff like, "That picture is so old," meaning "that movie," or when she says "I don't like that record," meaning "I don't like that song." Now, when it comes to grades or cleaning her kitchen "the Opal Jones" way she throws a messing fit. But, all in all, she's like my best friend.

My dad is up to par with my generation. My dad knows all of the latest hip hop news and sometimes more than I do. But when it comes to me hanging out with friends, everything changes. His rule is that I can only go out every once in a while, not every weekend. "You don't need to be goin' somewhere every weekend. Stay at home sometimes." This is what he says now that my brother has gone to college. But when my brother or boyfriend comes home, I can go anywhere as long as I am going with them. I think this is totally unfair, but all I can do is deal with it.

My middle brother and I are very close because we're close in age. We hang out together, and we basically have the same friends. Sometimes he can get on my nerves, but what siblings don't get on each other's nerves. He's the reason I met my boyfriend and I thank him for that. We have a good time every time we hang out.

My oldest brother and I were 14 years apart, so we didn't hang out much until he came back from college. He always used me to pick up girls. They would say, "Oh you're so sweet for taking care of your little sister," and then he would say something like, "Yeah, you know how I do." Then the next thing you knew they were giving him their numbers. Those girls were some dummies because they fell for it every time. He had this smile that could make me laugh when I was mad as hell. I don't know why, but it was just something about that smile. He died when I was in the eighth grade. It was a hard time for my family and me, especially my mom. But I think this tragedy made us stronger and closer. We cherish the moments that we have and we spend more time together.

My Chicks

What would a teenager do without friends? I would probably go insane. I have a variety of friends, so there is always something new to talk about – like what was on T.V. last night, who won the after-school fight and gossiping about others. Everyone talks about someone – it's human nature. But my two best friends are the ones that mean the most to me. They're my "ride or die" chicks. We do everything together and I mean everything. We have the same exact class schedule which means we're together all day. So, you hardly ever see one of us by ourselves. Around school we are known as The Triplets, Three Stooges and The Mean Girls. But we call ourselves the Sexy, Tenacious, Dudettes. We all have boyfriends, but we go out when we have the chance. When we get together, we go somewhere like the movies, to dinner or over to each other's houses. No matter what we do we always have fun. They would probably describe me as mean because I don't take crap from anyone. If someone presses the wrong button then I'll let them have it. They would also say that I always try to cheer them up. I hate to see people sad so I take it upon myself to show them my million dollar smile. That makes everyone happy.

Too young and Too Fly

From reading this you might think that I want to be a model or run track in the future because I'm so successful at it. But that's where you're wrong. This

57

is just something I do to keep myself busy, to stay out of trouble and to meet new people. My real goals are to graduate from high school and go to college on a scholarship. I want to major in nursing with a minor in psychology. Right now I am too focused on accomplishing my goals to worry about having a family, children, and a big house. Those things will come later on in life when I am done focusing on me. I'm too young and too fly for all of that right now...

ALICIA CASTILLO

Desperate Times Call for Desperate Measures

It's her first day at James Thomas High. The principal gave her a map, but she couldn't read it. As she was walking, she asked a boy by the name of Mark, where Room 614 was. He told her. He then asked whether she was a new student. She said that she transferred from school in Florida because her mother got a promotion. He thought that it was cool that she lived in Florida. He walked her to class. By lunch time, Jaylyn looked for Mark. When she found him she noticed he was drawing something. She said, "What are you drawing? It looks really cool?"

He said, "I'm drawing you a better map because the one you have is hard to make out." Jaylyn was so happy because she had made her first friend. Pretty soon the day was over and she walked home. After some weeks, things calmed down and she got used to things that were going on.

But one day while Mark and Jaylyn were eating lunch something unexpected happened. A group of girls walked by and one of the girls said, "Gross, I didn't know they let whales in." It was obvious the girl was talking about Jaylyn. Now Jaylyn had always been a little on the chubby side, but she never let it get to her as much as it did that day.

Later that night Jaylyn decided to go on a diet, where she only ate one meal a day, and she only drank liquids. Months went by, and she lost a lot of weight. She lost so much weight that she started getting sick. She was pale and weak looking, but she didn't care as long as she was skinny.

Weeks later she found herself getting a lot of attention. After school she was invited to a party. Jaylyn had never been invited to a party or anything, so she happily accepted.

Jaylyn decided to go on a crash diet where she didn't eat anything. She was scared that she would gain all her weight back. A couple weeks went by and it was time for the party.

The night of the party Jaylyn's mother came in and found her lying on the bed. She wasn't dead, but she was close to it. Her mother rushed her to the hospital. The doctors informed her that Jaylyn was suffering from anorexia.

59

They tried to feed her, but since her body had been deprived of food for so long, it now rejected it. The doctors said if she didn't eat she would die. Her mother couldn't believe that she would do something so stupid.

Meanwhile, Jaylyn told her mother in a faint voice if anything happened, to read her journal. Inside there were things. Like, "I hate myself!" and "beauty = skinny." As she read on she found out that Jaylyn hadn't been eating for months. Her mother sat on Jaylyn's bed and just cried. Jaylyn was her only child.

So you see, you shouldn't let people determine how you should look, dress, or act. As long as you love yourself other people will too. Jaylyn had an eating problem, but there are other problems teenagers face. If people don't like you for who you are then you don't need them. Be yourself and you will be just fine.

The Model in Me

I used to hear "Do you model?" a lot. I finally took interest in modeling when I was around 11 or 12 years old. Modeling looked fun, so I told my mom, and, of course, she said "okay." She was talking with one of her clients who had read about Barbizon, France. When she was coming home, she saw a building called "Barbizon," so she went in to see what they did. Barbizon happened to be a modeling school and agency. She remembered me telling her about modeling, so she asked about their next model call. I went to the call and got accepted.

I kept thinking, "Yes! I'm going to be a model and I'm going to get my hair done and look like Tyra Banks every day for school." But, it wasn't that easy. I had to attend school at Barbizon for a year. I learned good etiquette, how to walk, how to talk, and how to carry myself in a respectable way. Since graduating from Barbizon, I have been in about six fashion shows, one hair show, and two photo shoots. My mom told me not to make a big deal of it, not to tell my friends and put it in people's faces. But, modeling is a hobby for me – not a career – because by the time I'm twenty-four, they'll be looking for that "new face."

Interior decorating won't be just a hobby for me; it'll actually be my career. Modeling is about your outside beauty. Interior design is about how you feel, your visions, your personality. When I model, someone just says "put your hair like that, and go." It's just how they want me to look. Interior designing lets me decorate a house the way I want it to look, even though when I'm doing someone else's house, I'll be doing what they want.

In a way it's a metaphor. I want to build my house, and then create the inside of it. That's my way of expressing things. I want to do the whole three-sixty, not just paint it, like I would paint myself, put clothes on, makeup, then get out there and model. I want to actually build something. If you look at someone's house, you can see what kind of person they are. Some are junky, some are neat; some people don't care.

To create a house, first you have to have a vision. Then you make a blue-print of it. Then you get the supplies; you create the foundation; then you

61

build the house. When the house is built you paint it on the inside and on the outside, you put the furniture and appliances in, and then you decorate. To have a vision, I would need to know your interests, what you like, what excites you, your background, if you like outdoor things, indoor things, if you like to be with people or by yourself. I would need to know what's important in your life, what things you cannot live with and things that you need in your surroundings. I would have to know how you feel about things. I'm building a person, except not a person, a house: a person within a house. Your house should express you.

I'm walking in my house. There are big stairs – I don't even know why they're that big – they're like half of my height in width (I'm 5'8"). They're wooden, but you can't see the wood because there's carpet on them, cream-colored, like the walls. My living room is more to the right than to the left; it's almost in the center. You can't see all of the living room. I don't want people seeing into my house. My house is contemporary with two stories because I need space. Contemporary means lots of windows, not too big or small. My house will have lots of windows because I like saving electricity. I'll open the windows in the daytime. My mom taught me to do that.

When you walk in, the walls are cream-colored. It's very homey looking. There's a kitchen. I don't really like cooking; my mom does all that stuff, so maybe I'll have her live with me. The kitchen is big. I like big kitchens. I like the island in the middle because it's cute. I see a lot of new appliances just because they look good. The whole house is brownish because I like those colors – they look best on me, and they bring my mood down so that I'm not so extra-hyper. Blue makes you feel down, brings you down. Red makes you feel frustrated and angry. Yellow makes you high off of life. Yellow makes me dizzy. Brown brings me to where I'm cool. I'm right where I need to be.

The guest room is by the living room. There's a bathroom on the first floor. There's an office down there too. It's on the other side of the living room. The living room is the central room of the house. The office is mine, I'm mostly in there, but sometimes I go to see how my companies are doing. It's going to be a big, BIG office because my husband will be a businessman, with his own side. And it's going to be clean. I'll have a big bookshelf and in the corner, I'll have my little computer on an L-shaped computer desk. My kids are not allowed in the office because they'll mess everything up, so the door is closed. They'll be with a babysitter or something.

From the office I look at the backyard. The window takes in almost the whole yard. This is the only room that's not brown; it's black and "corporate" looking because I have to be in my business mode. The desks are wooden, but very corporate. The walls are nothing too dark because I'll fall asleep, but nothing too light because it just won't look good with my floors.

I'll have five bedrooms because I'll have three little kids by then, and one guest room, like for my mom maybe. All the bedrooms are upstairs, except the guest room is downstairs, because my guests will need their space. I want my family around me – in case anything happens – so their bedrooms are upstairs. There's a bedroom to the left, and a bathroom to the right, and the other three bedrooms are also to the right with a little playroom. The bedroom on the left is mine because I've got to be away from those kids. The kids are over there and they have their own little bedrooms. The kids aren't far from me; they're just not next to me.

The entire house is big, spacious, cozy, calm, and quiet, but not that quiet because I've got kids. Our house is clean with maybe a couple of toys lying around. Outside there's a big pool, one that you can gradually walk into, like at a beach. The deeper end is like a waterfall. No, that's not right; it's just the deeper end – no waterfall. The other part of it is the Jacuzzi. The kids aren't allowed in the Jacuzzi because they're kids and don't know anything about that type of stuff. There's a playground outside for the kids. I won't be out there that much because I'll be too busy.

The house is somewhere out there. There's a house that's for me. I don't know where that is. It's like I want so much, but there's nowhere that's exactly there for me. That's part of the reason why I have to build it. It's also why I want to make it for me, from the ground up. Just for the experience and because I don't think there's any place that is exactly for me.

I'm so confusing. I just have so much stuff. I'm trying to figure myself out. I feel confused. I don't want too many people to know about me until I figure myself out. I want people to understand that I do have dreams, and the truth is I don't know how I'm going to do this in my life. I just don't know how to get it. I need help. I want it. It's there.

Taking Matters Into My Own Little Hands

It would be so wonderful to just be performing on the stage without any criticism at all. That's one of the best parts, just to dance carefree. There would only be you, the stage, and the stage lights. No one would judge you. You would hear the music and do incredible moves that even amazed you. It would be like a dream world of your own where you would control everything. It's just a wonderful feeling. But this feeling for me had to come to an end.

My first ballet class was hard. The first time I walked into a dance studio I was nervous. It was a new environment and the only person I knew was my younger sister, Khadijah. I was nine years old and my sister was six years old. We were really tiny for our age, so it looked like I was six and she was three. Me and my little sister and I were new to the class and a little shy.

To get ready for our first ballet class we had to go downstairs to the locker rooms. The locker room itself was very big with soda and snack machines. The lockers were small and gray and packed on top of each other. Since Khadijah and I were so small, we used the closest locker at the bottom. We both had pink leotards and pink leggings with pink ballerina shoes. We went shopping and we picked out all the pink because that's my favorite color and it was very cute. After we changed my mother walked us up a flight of stairs and around two corners to the dance room.

There were lots of girls my age there with their parents. In the classroom was a wall made of a mirror, and a piano, a desk, and the ballet bars. Everything was clean and it looked so new. I was so excited. All that excitement led me to meeting my dance teacher. I was expecting a middle-aged woman in her later twenties or early thirties. But instead, I had a man teacher! He was very handsome and young. He looked like he was either twenty-one or twenty-two years old. His name was Rob, and he wore a tank top with leggings and dance shoes. He looked ridiculous, but he had a nice hair cut. He looked like he could be a metrosexual.

As soon as Rob came into the classroom some of the girls were saying his name, "Rob," so I figured they all knew him. My sister and I were still feelin' shy, so we kissed our mother goodbye and went into the room full of strangers.

The first thing we did in class was stretches. We got on the floor and spread our legs out to get more flexible, then we moved on to the next activity. We went to the ballet bar and learned more stretches. After that we learned a few ballet moves like the five positions, plié and how to relieve. There were like fifteen to twenty girls in the class so we were kind of squashed together for an hour and a half. After warm-ups, we had freestyle time to show off. I did a cartwheel and a Chinese split (oh yeah!). My sister did the same thing.

That day was hard. Making friends wasn't easy as it was at school. The girls were mean and jealous toward me and my little sister. The girls were like the "cool girls" in high school. We never really exchanged words, but our looks meant everything and we hated each other. I was too scared to say anything and my little sister was just mute back then. So words were never said, but I thought they were teacher's pets and I couldn't stand that!

I didn't really want to go back after that day, but I did. Each dance class got better, but the meaner the girls were, the more I didn't want to go back. I kept going anyway. I believe what kept me going back was actually performing the dances. I think that's the best part of being a dancer: presenting your good moves.

The last day of class for me and Khadijah was on a Saturday morning. By that time, I had really gotten tired of going, so I decided to take matters into my own little hands. When we got in the classroom, Rob started class. We did our stretches and learned more ballet moves and then it was time for freestyle. Throughout the whole process I was acting up and just way out of my character. I was not doing anything he told me to do. We were supposed to leap over pictures, but I decided to do cartwheels and slide over the pictures. That was my way of acting up in ballet class.

I guess it was pretty bad because Rob made me sit down until my mother came. He told her how I was acting up and she gave me a look that made me cry because I knew I was in trouble. Then my mother said "goodbye" and I apologized and we left. We got in the car and my mother asked me what was wrong with me. I told her how I didn't want to go back to dance class and she said she wouldn't make me.

It was hard to leave because I loved dance, but it was for the best until I could deal with criticism from my peers. I didn't want to deal with ballet for awhile, so I decided to act up. After that, I promised myself that I wouldn't let people get the best of me anymore and "to never settle for less, unless it's my best."

My freshman year in high school I went back to dancing. I missed performing and showing off my talent so I took it up at my school. It doesn't even compare to my old ballet class. I love what I'm doing. I love the instructor and my dance mates. Also, criticism isn't that bad either. It actually helps me, rather than making me mad.

Musician's Notes

Born into music – in my soul
In my mother, my grandmother
Singing gospel music in church
I was given the gift of music
Born to sing
Started playing the drums at four years old
Singing and playing drums at the same time
Joy, confidence
I learn something new every time I play
Life is stressful – can't wait to get to my drum set.

When I am away from music I feel lost
Music is a gift from God.
It changes people's lives, helps people.
Football will not make you as big a legend as music.
I choose music over football.
Marching Band members do better than the football players do.
You get a lot of credit when you play in the band.

Music will change you.
It will open your eyes.
Get you looking at the brighter side of life. Music is relaxing.
Music has you thinking about what is going on in the world.
See the world in a different perspective.
Songwriting. Sit back and express how you feel.

One time, a lot going on in my life, too busy to hang with myself.
Music helps you organize your life.
Drums and timing of music.
Keeping the beat straight with my girlfriend.
I don't know what to do –
playing drums would get my mind off of that –
make you know that everything will be all right.

My grandmother, mother, and aunt were very musically inclined. They were, and still are, well known around the state, let alone the country. Laura French, Monica Bohlen, and Emma French. Even though my grandmother is gone, people still recognize her in her children and grandchildren. My mom is a great singer and piano player. My aunt is also a phenomenal singer. To this day, everywhere we go someone knows us or knows about them.

Then the second generation came along. My aunt loves to sing around the house. Everytime I'm over there she sings me a little something just to make my day go better. When she is feeling bad I sing to her. When my grandmother passed, my aunt felt so bad. Me being the sweet five-year old, I would cheer her up. In November of 2006, my aunt recorded her first CD and I got the privilege to sing background for her.

As I got older music has always been there for me. In middle school I was a very bad student. I flunked the seventh grade and did a lot of bad things. It wasn't until my second semester as a seventh-grader when I discovered that music was what would keep me going. My band director, Stanley Coleman, helped me along the process. He always had me with the jazz band or the marching band.

My eighth grade year, two of the former members of the jazz band who were in high school asked me to be the drummer of their jazz trio. It lasted until last year when we broke up. But that didn't stop me from still loving what I do, and that's playing the drums in the band. I love what I do and I always will.

I can say that when I'm on a drum or close to one I feel so relaxed. The drums are my medicine. If I'm feeling ill, the worries and cares of life just fade away so swiftly. When I get on, it's just me and my drums going at it. I can imagine my problems being solved through that. It takes my mind away from lots of crap that has happened in my past life or in my present life. I really can't see myself without music at all.

Drums are one of the best things to happen to me since my girlfriend. I play the drums every chance I get. Being that I'm so busy, I barely have time to practice. I play in two bands. One of the bands is out of school and one is in school. I've played in both bands for quite some time.

I plan to get scholarships and go to college for music. I hope to get adequate in music education and music business. Maybe if the jazz bands stay together we could play in places we would never imagine.

ERIC OLIVER

HIP HOP E-ROC

I was born April 6, 1990. That's ten years after my guidance counselor was created. The late 70's early 80's is when HIP-HOP was born.

Now I ain't finna to go into the whole history about it because let's be honest, it's about me – me and my relationship with HIP-HOP as of the year 2006. If you were paying attention and can add, I'm 16 now. I'm at that point in age where I'm growing into a full adult. Being a black male, I was told from the jump about bumps and bruises I was going to receive through my life obstacles.

And that right there is like the whole point of me talking. The contract between my parents and "legal" parents. My "legal" parents lecture. My parents converse. You know how when a loved one dies and they say they are with you in spirit? My parent, HIP-HOP is always with me. Mom and Dad can't be with you wherever you go. But G-Unit clothing is on my chest when I party. A Young Jeezy CD is with me while I walk. A Jay-Z video is playing in a sports bar. As of 2006, HIP-HOP has become if not America's culture, the world's subculture.

Let's be honest, the only thing stopping it from taking over, is the fact it's led by a minority group of men, none other than the blacks. Pimping was legal until black men started making a profit off it. Cocaine was ok until black men started making a profit off it. Coke only became ok when it started getting cooked. Thus allowing crack to kill the black communities like the plague. A drug in which even the CIA was thought to take part in, but that's a different subject.

I'm talking about the life of HIP-HOP. The one that's in millions of others just like me. HIP-HOP surpasses rhymes on a beat to me. It's my clothing, my vocab, my swagger, my train of thought. It dictates the crowd I hang around, the codes that I follow. All which my mama couldn't tell me in 16 years. They always wanna talk about the negatives that come with it. Do you know how many anger management classes I didn't have to attend? Life altering classics like 50 Cent – *Get Rich or Die Trying*; Lil Wayne – *Tha Carter*; Ludacris – *Back for the First Time*, *nawmsayin*. Being a small cat out here when everyone seemed big I felt no one was understanding the respect I was trying to establish. Till I heard

"Born in the city were the skinny n***** fry/ and as a skinny n**** I had beef with high size." - Jay Z *"Diamonds is Forever"*

I was like, "Yeah that's what I been tryna' get through to these dudes."

And then right when I thought that was enough, I got a dose of aggression when I heard the same line but flipped different.

"In the city were the skinny n***** die (nope)/ it's the city were the skinny n***** ride (yeah)." - Juelz Santana *"Dipset Anthem"*

I can't even begin to tell you the times where rap done got me out of trouble. I mean, hip-hop constructed my whole mind frame. Contrary to your beliefs, my lifestyle isn't anything like my favorite rappers. Most rappers sold drugs, did bids, "bust guns," living in a poverty stricken area. Me, I'm from University City, St. Louis, Missouri, the county. Police patrol the streets. It's kind of segregated. The majority of whites stay on the south side of Olive Boulevard while the majority of blacks stay on the north side of the street. Drugs float around but what can I say, weed is universal. To make a long story short, my living conditions are where they should be. I don't get into trouble, I don't smoke or drink. I'm more intelligent than you think. I guess I don't have on the proper attire for you to think otherwise.

Don't judge me. Then again this life is nothing but judges and verdicts for me, I can't help that. I won't help that. This is me everyday.

Life Through Music

My passion for playing the clarinet is so strong that I even play in my sleep. Playing the clarinet gives me an indescribable feeling. I love this feeling and I also release stress when I play my instrument. The clarinet has been a part of my life since the seventh grade and it led me to joining a band, being selected into different bands, meeting new people, being able to travel, and becoming a leader. It's so cool to hear more experienced bands and all the different in- struments. Playing the clarinet and being in a band is my life and its friggling awesome. I thrive off of it.

It all started when I was in the seventh grade at the Brittany Woods Middle School. My sister, Ashley, was in band; we're two years apart. She used to play clarinet. I needed something to do so I just joined the band. At first I just wanted to play the trumpet, but people told me it was a boy instrument. I was mad because I really wanted to play the trumpet. And, I didn't like the flute because it was too small, so I ended up with the clarinet. I liked the sound of the instrument because I heard Ashley play it before.

I was in beginning band. I was bored in class because I was a fast learner and the other people weren't. So I just started helping other people and playing different notes on my instrument to see how they sounded. My mom rented me an instrument over the summer before I started class. Ashley had an instru- ment, but it got stolen at the high school, so we had to share. Then, later into school my band teacher gave me another instrument. My original instrument was really old and rusty but I was still proud of it. The clarinet my band director gave me was real shiny and looked fairly new. It felt and played very smooth.

At first it was frustrating, but it pushed me because I thought why doesn't mine make the same sound like Ashley's? I later found out that I wasn't the best, which shocked me, because at first I thought I was. It took me a couple of months of practice and disciplining myself, but I did get better. I had outside help from my sister but she started to misuse her authority so I just began to teach myself. I was supposed to move into intermediate band, but I couldn't because it conflicted with my schedule. So instead of changing my schedule I remained in beginning band until the year ended and joined advanced marching band in the eighth grade.

High School

The summer before I entered ninth grade, I went to band camp which was hectic because I was in a new surrounding filled with new people. Band camp was the worst. We had to do a lot of physical exercises which included six inches[1], push ups, running around the school building, and pet the dog[2] which in my opinion is the worst exercise. I was thinking to myself, "Are they crazy? Do they feel this heat? What are they thinking?" We had to break up into sectionals.[3] I hated this because in sectionals all we did was additional exercises. This drove me insane and they would try to get in my face, but my attitude was too bad for them, so we always got into arguments. The thought of quitting even crossed my mind, but I decided I would not going to pleasure them by quitting something I enjoyed.

After band camp ended, the school year began and things calmed down a lot. My first day in class was slow because we came to class, took our instruments out, and sat and waited for the teacher to take attendance. We eventually played through some music from band camp. I thought I was the perfect player, but then I heard the upperclassmen playing and I thought. Wow, I really need to practice. I wanted to be the best. As the band director passed out music, and I saw the high notes, I didn't know the clarinet could go that high. Amazed. At first it was different, but I stuck with it. By sticking to it and my determination, I finally got it.

Then I started out playing first clarinet and I had adopted a "big sister" in band. Her name was Kortney House. Kortney was very nice to me and helped me in class when I asked about notes. She never told me if I annoyed her. She was one of my favorite upperclassmen because she didn't act snobby or like she was better than anybody. She was one of the only people who took the time to help me. I thought she was a very good person and I thank her for that.

1 In this exercise you have to lie on your back and raise your legs approximately six inches above the ground and hold in until the person giving the exercise says, "down."

2 In this exercise you have to extend your arms and you clap them above your head but you can't bend your elbows and every ten counts you have to hold your arms out and either bark like a dog, snap your fingers, or make the kissing noise that you make to dogs to dogs.

3 Sectionals are when people in band break up into groups, consisting of people that play the same instrument; examples would be all clarinets, trumpets, flutes, drummers, etc., going into separate rooms to practice on any necessary things. (Music, marching, chants, etc.)

Band Trips

My first band trip out of town was the best. We went to Little Rock Arkansas and were in UAPB's, (University Arkansas Pine Bluff), homecoming parade and it was totally awesome. It is amazing to go to another city and see people crowded everywhere around congratulating and cheering for you. Let me remind you that we were not in St. Louis and these people didn't know anything about us, but they were still ecstatic to see us perform. It was incredible Parades down there are nothing like parades here, there are way more people to go out to the parades and cheer the performers on than here. Parades are huge! I was so scared to see all those people. I thought I was going to forget my music or I was going to get off step. In my mind a million things could've went wrong, but they didn't. People kept coming up to us congratulating us and telling us how good we sounded. I was so happy.

On my second band trip, I was happy because this trip is what band member's look forward to each year. We were going to Indianapolis, Indiana, for the Circuit City Classic parade and game. This is a major classic; it's similar to the Gateway Classic and bigger. It was amazing! The bands and the people were so hyped and active in the performances. After the parade was game time. I was so anxious for half-time so that I could see the many formations that these two bands came up with. Their performances were great and the crowd was going crazy! Once the field show was over I was ready to go but I wasn't able to because some people wanted to watch the game.

My junior year we went on two band trips: Jackson State University and Lincoln University. The first trip we went on was to Lincoln; it was an okay trip. We left early that morning and returned late that night. Once we got to Lincoln we had to rush to put on our clothes because we didn't wear our clothes on the bus. The parade was fun and we basically marched around the school. The only thing I didn't like was that Jefferson City has a lot of hills. We marched up, then back down, then up again, just to go right back down the hill. It was very nerve-wracking.

On the second trip of my junior year, we went to Jackson, Mississippi. We left early that morning and we were on the road the majority of the day, except for short stops to eat. We spent our first day at the pep rally and the next day we marched in the homecoming parade. The parade was extremely long, but I made it through it. We went through a tunnel and it was amazing. We sounded magnificent. This was one of those things that you had to be there to understand the feeling.

When we finished marching in the parade, we played one song in the parking lot and then we were allowed to go back and watch the rest of the parade. The parade was so cold so some friends and I asked a policeman if we could sit in the back of the police car and we did. The game was ridiculously cold too and I fell asleep. I woke up just in time to see the halftime show. Their theme that year was "throwback" and they had alumni dancers and drum majors. They had a football field full of people. They split the dancers up into three groups: past, present and future. It was great they had these little girls down there dancing making some older people who claimed to be dancers look stupid. They had some thirty and forty-year-old men and women on the field dancing like they were in their teens. Still it was marvelous. I wish I could see that show again. I haven't seen any show better than that one 'til this day.

Junior year

Playing the clarinet in high school has opened more doors for me. I've become a section leader. It's sad to say, but I barely take my instrument home now. I used to practice at least once every two days. I only practice a week before an event or I don't at all, but I had to start back practicing daily because I had to practice for a selective band. I was very excited about that because I feel I worked very hard for it and wanted to excel in it.

The performance took place at UMSL, University of Missouri St. Louis, and it was mixture of different students from different bands. We were there for the whole day and practiced from eight o'clock that morning until a little after four that evening. The performance did not start until six that evening and I was so scared that I was going to mess up because I messed up a few times in practice. I was mad because they made me play third clarinet and I felt so degraded. I told my band teacher and he said, "If you practice more then maybe next year you will play first."

Over Thanksgiving break I thought I was going to die because I went out of town and didn't go to school a few days before so I didn't play for like a week and a half and I told my ma' that I totally missed my clarinet. I couldn't wait to get back to school, but we had a substitute so we couldn't play. I was depressed. I learned from that and when spring break came my instrument was right at home with me. I would rather be playing my instrument than going to some of my other boring classes. When I'm in some classes I can't wait to get to band so I can play.

I haven't stopped playing my clarinet, but I have started to learn the flute and bass clarinet. I went back to my old dream of playing the trumpet, but the band director didn't have one for me to use, so again, that dream was crushed. One day I'm going to master a trumpet. I don't practice the flute anymore because it was of no interest to me, but I do still play the bass clarinet. At first I hated it because I was never heard, it was extremely low and I couldn't play, I was always squeaking. I kept playing and I went to my band director in study hall and he helped me with notes and rhythms.

Band has taken me a lot of places geographically and mentally. It has taken me to Jefferson City, Missouri; Indianapolis, Indiana; Jackson, Mississippi; and Little Rock, Arkansas. Mentally, band has allowed me to mature as a person giving me more discipline. Band will always be a part of my life in some way. I haven't made up my mind whether or not I'm going to do band in college, but it's still an option. Band has groomed my personality with determination, higher confidence, optimism, and passion. Through band I have learned to make my own choices and to live my life for me and not for others.

After participating in band for all these years I have other dreams to accomplish. I want to attend a competitive university and if I get accepted I will have to put band on hold for a while but it will always be a part of me. This is me:

"I won't give up. I can't give up. I will never fail. They can't hold me down."

I Am My Own Competition

I'm on a track, but it is unfamiliar to me. The pavement is jet black with thick white lines stretching as far as I can see. I take the inside lane because it's the easiest. If I just stay right there on that path, I might have a chance.

The girl in the next lane is a mirror image of me. She is my greatest competition. We look exactly the same, but we're different. That person is the person other people see in me, but I don't see in myself. This person is the person I want to be. People say to her, "Oh, you're so smart. You're gonna' make it." But the person I see is going to fail. I'm not good enough.

I'm not going to win the race. I want to win, but I'm okay at everything and never the best at anything. So my main competition is me. I am not the last person, but I am not the first. I am in the middle. The other competition feels like everyone, everyone else in the world. I'm racing against the people I go to school with, and then my family. I'm racing against my family because I want to do something with my life. My family didn't go to college. Their jobs (my aunts, my dad, my mom) consist of maintenance and food service. I feel like they're going to lose the race. Except my mom. She's a strong woman and has to work extra hard to get to the finish line. I don't want to struggle like her. Even though I might win compared to my family, it's not good enough. I might end up just like them.

The gun goes off and I feel my heart drop. I hear the gun and I know it's time. This is it. I have to do this right because if I don't I'll fail. I'm going to lose. I'm running in the race, with the goal of getting first place. My leg muscles are strained, sweat drips down my face, making it difficult to see and I experience shortness of breath. Yet, I have to keep going. I HAVE TO WIN! I want to give up because it HURTS SO BAD, but if I give up, I'll be a LOSER! I HAVE TO BE FIRST! I have to win the race. For me, being last is unacceptable and being in the middle is simply not good enough. Sometimes the race seems so long, that I think that I'll never be able to finish it. I can barely see the finish line. It's blurry. I might get there – stagger in and stumble, but it's not going to be where I want to be. The fact that I constantly doubt myself and question my abilities, keeps me from winning the race. I am my own competition.

There's this constant juggle and weight on my shoulders. I have to do well in school (all A's), talk to my friends (maintain a social life), study for upcoming tests, search for colleges (where do I begin and how do I go about it?), boys (self-explanatory), remember important dates, keep in touch with my family (my brothers and my dad), buy clothes (which is extremely depressing at times, especially when shopping for jeans), go to work (I can't quit because I have to pay my cell phone bill and get the things I want.) It starts to weigh me down and I drop a few things, and I want to stop and pick them up, but then I'll get further behind. I have to go to church (read the Bible, pray and exhibit my Christianity throughout my everyday life). Will the list ever end? My back begins to hurt from all the weight. There's always something to do, say and even hear; everything has to be done and it has to be done RIGHT! I try to do everything everyone expects me to do. It seems like people are constantly getting on me about preparing for college, getting good grades, getting involved. Then there are my friends whose main concerns are boys and shopping. In elementary school, people didn't think about college, but I did. So I kept my grades up, but nobody ever looks at elementary or middle school. I don't know. I guess it's all part of growing up.

I try to keep going and I want to get to the other girl that others see who is me. I want to be equal to her and that's how I want to be, but I don't think that I'm on her level. Then as I'm running I see others pass me by and I get discouraged and I think I'm not going to make it. Now I can't even see the finish line. There are people in the stands, but I can't see them. Everyone who has encouraged me in my life is there too, on the side by the finish line because that's where they said I'm going to be; they believe I'm going to make it. I know that everything I do, I have to do it now, or else I will fail. My life seems so complicated that I can't even write everything down. My thoughts are so jumbled and I can't figure out which direction I'm going. There's so much to do and it seems like there's not a lot of time.

I want to run a different race. I want to be the person that everyone else sees. It has a lot to do with confidence. I have more confidence in other people than myself. I think they can be successful, they can fail, but if I fail, it's not okay. If they fail, if they fall in the race, they can get back up.

I want to run a different race. Before they even shoot the gun, I'm confident. I have no doubts. I'm prepared. I'm ready. I'm not nervous. Get Ready. Get Set. Bang! I sprint forward fast, real fast. I'm pacing myself and I'm ready. I hear the crowd screaming my name and cheering me on from the front row of the stands. I feel the wind slightly blowing across my face. It's not against me. I'm not struggling. I know I'm going to win. I take long, even strides until I'm neck and neck with myself, ahead of everyone else. We get close to the end and I leap forward crossing the finish line. I win. I win happiness. That's my main goal.

Running For My Life

The third grade was the first time my brother and I ever ran a race. We had to race other people at school to see who would be on the team. My brother and I came in first and second. I don't even remember who was first. From that moment on we knew what we had was the best.

My relay team and I went to State with four of the fastest people in school, me included. We were about to run the 4x200 relay and as we walked to the start line I got into the block and the gun went up. I was running the first leg. The gun went off and right out of the blocks I was on a roll. I passed everyone in front of me. We got to the second runner and everything was still going okay. On to the third runner, which was my twin brother, and we were still in the top three. When we got to the last of our runners, his spike came through his shoe and he jumped in the air, so we knew something was wrong. We didn't know what had happened until the race was over. We finished a tenth of a second out of eighth place. As the race was over we all got back together as a team. Some were talking, but I wasn't. I called my mom and told her what happened and as I was telling her, I began to cry.

When I got to high school I didn't know what sport I wanted to play. My brother and I just tried out everything, and we played football for the first time ever. You would think the running back is the fastest on the team but he wasn't, my twin brother and I were. When it's time for college, we're going to go to the same place, and present ourselves as a package.

Now I run track. I run the 100m, 200m, 400m, and the 4x100m and 4x200m relays. As a freshman, I ran my 100m dash in 10.9 seconds and broke the school record. I don't run the 200m a lot, but when I do I can get like a 22.1 or lower if I run just a little bit faster. In my 400m, I run when I want to, and I get like a 51 or faster. I'm working on getting that time way down.

In the 100m dash a 10.9 is fast, but there is always faster. I broke the school record, which was 11.4 as a freshman, and if someone was to beat it, it would make me feel like they are better than me and faster than me so I would try to break their record. Right now I feel good that I hold the school record.

In the 2x100M I run with a team and we are the best in the school. Last year I wasn't really focused on running and that showed. I didn't make it to State and we lost districts. I made a lot of mistakes, such as dropping the baton, fooling around right before the race, and other things like that. I felt really bad because I let myself down and my family. I plan on running track this year because I want to get that fun feeling that I had as a freshman. I have two more years to do so. I know I'm going to get there.

Play Hard

It all started years back when I was about eleven years old. I was in middle school and I had no interest in basketball, even though I had a cousin who loved the game. No interest in basketball, but this cousin was my favorite. He was what you would call a straight hooper. I mean he was the full package. Jimmy was a star: a legend-to-be. I attended every one of his games, even his games out of state.

Since Jimmy McKinney was my favorite, I looked up to him as a role model. I wanted to be just like him and I even started to do the things he did. So, one day at school I saw this girl. I didn't know her from a can of paint. Something drew me to her. I'm not sure what, but when I saw her, I felt like she was going to be my friend. When I spoke to her she felt the same way. We began to talk and I told her stuff about me and she told me stuff about her. This girl's name was Ja'Vette and she was a wonderful friend; we even became best friends. As we were talking Ja'Vette mentioned basketball.

Instantly, I felt happy and said, "B-A-S-K-E-T-B-A-L-L! My cousin loved the game."

"Well, said Ja'Vette, "I was trying to tell you that I play."

"You do?" I replied.

Ja'Vette told me that I should come and play on her team. I told her that I would ask my mom. My mom said it was okay. Believe it or not we had practice the next day, and I was there, which was a Monday. We practiced every Monday and Wednesday at the Herbert Hoover Boys & Girls Club. On that first day Ja'Vette introduced me to the Coach. When I saw him I knew that he was a nice and open person. After being introduced Ja'Vette told him I was Jimmy's cousin.

"You, Jimmy's cousin?" Coach Darrin asked me.

"Yeeah," I said.

"Jimmy McKinney?"

"Yes, Jimmy McKinney."

Right then I thought to myself that everybody knew Jimmy and that, man, he had a good name. After our brief conversation, Coach Darrin told me to get in line. We started doing dribbling drills. Honestly, I never even knew what drilling was. I was up next and I wasn't very confident in drilling the boy up and down the court. Anyway, since I wasn't drilling I had no control over the ball. I kept on losing my dribble.

The only thing I could think was that I wanted to be like the other kids. In the sixth grade kids were good ball players. I was young and it was my first time ever playing, and these girls had been playing since the second and third grade. As a kid I didn't realize that I just wanted to be like everyone else. Even though I wasn't on the same level as the other players, that didn't stop me from working hard. I think it made me work even harder.

With inner confidence and the support of others, I still play basketball today. Basketball has been great because it was the key to finding Ja'Vette, an amazing person to be my best friend. Ja'Vette still is a great person; she's like a sister. She's smart and talented in many ways. We play basketball together at Career Academy for the Lady Phoenix.

As a freshman, I made the varsity team and at one point in the season, I even started. That was a great jump for me. With my determination, I became a great defensive player who has heart and the desire to win. Defense is my biggest strength, just as if something was someone's lifeline. I love defense. It's motivation. It's motivation because, for me, it hypes up the game. When I play defense I show no mercy. I leave it all on the floor and I don't regret my aggressive mentality. I love defense because it helps me release my energetic side. I also love it because it is fun taking the ball, blocking a shot, or shutting down a top scorer. Defense helps me be compatible, not only on the court, but also in the classroom. I just love it. It's a passion.

Although my role on the team is mainly defensive, I still help out on offense. I play two positions: small forward and shooting guard. I prefer small forward because I can drive and shoot the ball. I consider myself a playmaker.

My junior year started off great. I started again at small forward. Then, BAM! With a couple more season games left, I hurt my hand and missed about four games. My knuckle pushed back into the palm of my hand and I was in a lot of pain.

Jimmy, or as friends would say, "J-Roc," is overseas in Germany playing professional basketball. I do not speak to Jimmy as often as I used to. It's hard to keep in touch because of the time difference. When I'm awake, he is asleep, and when I am asleep, he is awake. When I was younger, Jimmy watched me play occasionally, but when I had high school games he was away for college playing for Missouri. Although he hasn't seen me play, over the summer, he worked with me and my cousin. Jimmy would tell us to go hard and be confident. Actually, I know he is proud of me, not only because of athletics, but also because of the academic side of me.

Although I love basketball, I have a greater passion for helping people in need. On the other hand, if basketball comes through for me, I would never turn down the offer. I know that I have to work hard and improve my skills to play on a Division I level. I know I need to improve, but there's nothing wrong with improvement. As a former Rams' football player recently said, "You know the largest room in the world?...The room for improvement."

My Turn Now

Smiling Brother (Pablo).
Lil' Pablo
Pablo Lil' Sis.
Pablo went to State.

Girl's suck. Boys are strong. (Showing boys wrong).
Tough, Strong, Exhausting, Running a lot.
Laughing, Playing, Fighting, Wrestling, Moving, Ducking.

Living up to big brother.

Starting Competition.
Teammates Encouraging, Clapping, Yelling, Arguing, Congratulating.
Districts, First Match. First year.

Feet, Legs, Arms, Neck, Moving, Quick, Fast, Blood, Sweat, Tears
Pain, Frustration, Strength, Aspiration
Relieved.

Bruises, Attacking, Exercising
Losing Weight, Gaining weight, Weight classes.

Being the best, Being like my brother, Being better than my brother.

Push-ups, Sit-ups, The box, Perfect stance
Commitment, No quitters, Never give up
Breathe evenly, Learning new moves
Need more strength!
Exercise now, Gain more muscle.
Show who's boss!

Good sportsmanship.
Win or lose. Lose not an option.
Focus on opponent's reaction.
Find opponent's weakness.
Focus, Focus, Focus!

Be stronger than your opponent.
Sore shoulders. Sore arms. Breaking point.
Outsmarting your opponent. Scoring your opponent.

I love my brother. Proud of my brother, but I want to do my thing.
My name is still Pablo's lil' sister or lil' Pablo.

My brother Pablo is 18 years old. He graduated from high school in 2006. Since he's in college now, I can wrestle. He didn't want me wrestling because . . . I actually don't know the reason. Pablo is a great wrestler. He wrestled since he was a freshman. Now it's my turn. I only wrestle boys. Some I win, some I lose. I love my brother and we are super close. My teammates call me "Lil Pablo" Pablo's lil sis, or they just say Pablo. I love sports so I just wanted to try something different.

I started wrestling when I was seventeen years old. I knew that it wasn't usual for a girl to wrestle, but I wanted to because all of the moves seemed so interesting, especially when they slammed people. I was so into it and I yelled and I screamed because it looked so fun.

I'm not the only girl on the team though, there are two other girls. People on the team say that I'm the strongest girl. They say I can overpower a lot of people on the team. A lot of boys are stronger that me, but if you don't know the technique, you won't win.

I'm not afraid to wrestle anyone. We have to run a lot. We run for thirty minutes. We also do push ups and sit-ups, stretches, and hand fighting exercises (moves using only our hands). We learn defensive and offensive moves. When we do those things, we're supposed to keep going and not stop.

If you do something wrong like stand there while everyone's practicing, call the coach by his last name, or talk while the coach is talking you get the box. The box is full of books and you have to do exercises with them. You have to lift the box over your head and do push-ups and sit-ups with it. It's so funny when people get sent to the box, they look so mad. But, when they get finished, they get to come back to practice and, hopefully, they learned their lesson. I've never gotten the box.

We have a certain stance. If you have the perfect stance it's harder for your opponent to take you down. You have to focus on your opponent and find their weakness when you get on the mat to go against them. You have to be quick and never give up.

82

More than likely you will come out with bruises. Some people have black eyes, sore body parts or cuts and scrapes. A lot of times you may see one person on one of the teams who has a bloody nose.

To win you have to believe in yourself and sometimes manipulate your opponent. You have to make him think that you are ready for the battle even if you are not. You also have to make sure you breathe evenly.

When I go out to wrestle, I laugh and smile. Wrestling is so fun to me, even though it's hard and challenging.

I know that I'm committed to the team. I had to wrestle for my starting spot. I can't believe I'm a girl and I started and it was only my first year. Even if I hadn't gotten a starting spot I wouldn't quit the team because I love it so much. I've played other sports in the past, but wrestling is one of my favorites.

Being a girl wrestler is hard. Peer pressure is there everyday. You get talked about because you are a female wrestler. You get called "gay" and a lot of other things. No one knows how I live my life so they can call me what they want because I know it's not true. The only people I'm worried about are my teammates because if I let the team down then I will be worried.

My motto is focus, focus, focus! Because if my mind's focused on other things while I'm in a match then I won't think quickly to react to my opponent's moves and I might not win. Since I'm a girl, my teammates want me to beat every boy I wrestle. Even if I don't beat them they still clap for me.

Sometimes I do have a breaking point. My breaking point is when I get my opponent in the position where I can win. I try even harder and when it looks like he is going to win it makes me try much harder than that. My shoulders and arms are always sore. I can feel my muscles getting stronger because things I couldn't do I can do now.

It was hard wrestling my first year, but I practiced hard and I did what I had to do. My work paid off when I beat a boy from Gateway High School. The score was 11 to 4, but even though I didn't pin him (even though I almost did), I outworked him and that's all that matters. I felt so excited and I proved my point when I won.

Pablo was proud of me, but he told me I need some help with technique. He said he would help me. He said that he couldn't believe that I wrestled like I did for my first year.

Next year I plan to wrestle again, but this time I will work even harder to keep my spot. Even though I didn't go to state like Pablo, I will try even harder to go next year. Trust me, it won't be the same.

For The Love Of The Game

In the mind of every little kid in Ghana is to be a very great soccer player in the world. Soccer is a game loved by the whole of Africa – especially where I come from, Ghana, on the west coast of Africa. Ronaldinho, Freddy Adu, Zinedin Zidane, and Therry Henry are the most celebrated soccer players in the world now and I think they all have a story to tell about their love for the game of soccer. I also have my own story to tell about the game I love and adore.

I started up with the same dream to play at the world front and to try to be the best that I can be. My mom even told me once to stop playing soccer and focus on my studies instead and get good grades. But I had to do anything else to play, even if I had to disobey my mom and sneak out to play and also make sure I returned before she came back home.

On one bright sunny Sunday, which was our game day, I met my friends outside my house for a game. And this was the most unfortunate day for me. Our little field was a dirt-filled park with scattered gravel. The field was lined with five trees on each side – the trees at the end of the field served as goal posts. As the trees were not planted accurately, some goals were wider than the others. This helped the team who got there first because they got to choose the smaller goal while the other team chose the larger goal. With this difference in goal size there was always arguing about goals since you couldn't prove if it was really a goal. Sometimes the goals were switched with medium or large slab bricks which were to be used for building new houses but we stole them from their building sites. This made it a little more challenging to score and we boosted our goal skills and shooting skills. So nothing on this field was regulation size.

As we were playing the game I was trying to pull off a trick to score my sixth goal of the day. I was tripped by someone on the other team and I fell and landed on a sharp-edged gravel on the ground and it cut deep into my left leg and blood started oozing out. I was taken home immediately and my mom was really mad at me for that and she threatened to beat me before attending to the wound. She later calmed down and treated it for me and told me not to leave the house again. But some few days later, as I felt better and the wound was healing, I sneaked out again when my mother went to market to get some groceries. And this is how the journey began.

From then on I was asked to play with the old folks and I got my first soccer shoes, and I also learned from this to be a more determined player. Because the old people on the main field don't care whether you are a kid or not and when they hit you they tell you to "Man-up" and this made me into a tough and strong player. With this experience I got, I play the game that I love with everybody from kids to adults and hope to be the best that I can ever be and be great in the game that I love, the beautiful game of the world, "Joga Bonito."

Leavin' It On The Field

Football clears my mind of what's going on and also lets me be as aggressive as I want to be. I started playing my sophomore year in high school. Before that, I played track and field. I decided to try football because my friends told me to try it and the coach talked to me. They thought I would be good at football because of my size. The summer before my sophomore year, I went to a football camp at Central Methodist College in Fayette, Missouri. We went through lots of drills and practiced against other teams from around the state. I wasn't that good at it at first, but I didn't want to give up. I didn't like quitting.

After camp, our football team worked out to prepare for the season. I got a bit better. During my first year I played defensive tackle and offensive guard. An offensive guard blocks the interior part of the line to protect the quarterback. The defensive tackle, which I like better, tries to stop the quarterback from throwing the ball and tackles anyone with the ball running through the middle. I love the contact and loud bang of the pads when they hit each other.

I grew to love the sport. One day I want to be able to play college football. I just need to grow a little bit more. Football helps me free my mind and get rid of anger and feelings that I have that I just can't get rid of. They are stuck in the back of my mind. I am afraid of what will happen just expressing my thoughts. So football lets me unleash my anger and frustration about some of the things that go on in my life and at home. It's basically a peaceful place for me to be, like when I sleep and have a dream.

Instead of putting my thoughts down with pen and paper, I find it more relaxing to leave it all on the field. It lets me be as physical as I want to be. That is why I also enjoy lifting weights so much because I can put my frustration in the weights. When I want to get that last little push, my thoughts encourage me to do more. I just love how free it makes me feel and I know that it does nothing but help me. It can actually get me somewhere in life. That's why when my next season comes around I will play my heart out and do the best that I know I can.

Never Give Up

It all started when I was seven years old, playing football for Herbert Hoover Boys and Girls Club. I had got introduced to the club and football because my big cousin, Demarco, played football for the Boys Club. I played quarterback and linebacker. I played at Herbert Hoover for six years, until I was thirteen years old. Every year I had a winning season, except our team lost the Super Bowl (all the St. Louis junior football league teams) ever year until we were thirteen. Out of all my years at Herbert Hoover, our team won one Super Bowl, two national championships (in Daytona Beach, Florida with teams from around the country), and I earned a couple of MVP trophies. After my last season at Herbert Hoover, I was happy that I was about to play high school football.

When I got to high school at Career Academy, it was the school's first year of varsity football. I was excited that I was going to be part of history because it was the school's first-ever varsity football team. I worked very hard to get a starting position at cornerback on defense. I really thought we were going to have a nice team, but we didn't. We went 0-10 and didn't score in any games, not even one. We still had fun because we were doing something we loved to do, and because we knew we were a young team with all freshmen and sophomores. That summer we went to all kinds of football camps – at Mizzou and Southern Illinois University-Edwardsville – to lift weights and get bigger.

The next season, my sophomore year, I got the starting spot at cornerback again. We started off the same way we did last season: losing. In the middle of the season, we won our first game in school history. The next week we played one of the best teams in our conference and lost in overtime 14 to 13. We were sad that we lost, but we were proud too because we played a very good game against a very good team. After that game we went back on another two game losing streak. When districts started, we were a totally different team. We won our first district game, but lost our next game. That next week, we played on the best teams in our Class 3 football division and we won. We didn't win districts, but we did a good job at the end of the season. That made us work even harder over the summer.

The next season, my junior year, started and I got my starting spot at cornerback again. We won our first game of the season by a score of 8 to 6, and we were very excited about the win. But, then we lost our next three games, even though the scores were close. We won our next two games and after that, we played one of the best teams in the conference and lost a heartbreaker, 13 to 12. We were still proud of each other.

When districts started, we had won all three games and we won our first district football title in school history. After districts, the playoffs started. We won our first playoff game ever in school history and we made it to the second round of the playoffs. We lost in the second round and finished the season with a 7-5 record. Even though we lost that last game, we felt good because we accomplished a lot of our goals.

I still have one year left of high school football to try to win a state title. I've learned to play as a team and to be like a family on and off the field. My football career at Career Academy has taught me to never give up at whatever I do.

What Is Love?

Love is dedication. Dedication is the focus on what you love. Your love is what you appreciate more than anything in this life. Some people love sports, exotic cars, money and music. Some just love to sit back and relax with family and friends. Me...I love my family, my friends and basketball. Personally, I can't live without passion and these are my passions: they are what I'm dedicated to and that's what I love.

I feel that in order to truly love, you must embrace everything you care about. I take my dedication to love and make it my inspiration to continue on. I realize not everyday is going to be sunshine; some days will include rain, sleet, snow and sometimes pure hail. On those days I just think about what I'm dedicated to and then I begin to love. I'm inspired to continue on trying until the forecast calls for sunshine.

Some days I'm tempted to quit. I feel as if I'm destined to fall then I stop and think, "If I fall, then what?" Who and what will I have become? What will life have to say? If I quit am I destined to fail?"

Sometimes I feel as if I have too many questions and not enough answers. If I do something negative I know that I am the one affected by my own actions or my inactions. If I fall I am the one responsible for getting back up and if I don't get back up then, DAMN IT, I better be dead. Once I'm inspired to do the most with what I have in order to establish my own legacy and write my own history without quitting, self-destructing, or for that matter following behind anybody. In the end my legacy will be whatever I have thought, said, and done.

To those who tell me I can't draw, I can't play basketball, or I've lost my ability to sit back and smile, I beg of you to keep on talking because I'm going to keep proving you wrong. Everything you say to me challenges me to be driven from within. Michael Jordan said it best "I've failed over and over again and that is why I will succeed." That is my definition of love.

That Would Be Yes

I am a junior in high school and every time I realize only one year is left for me, I get scared. I get scared because the ideas run through my mind like what college will I attend, how will I get the money, or am I ready? Sooner or later, I will be able to answer all these questions.

One way I'm looking to get to college is on an athletic scholarship. The sport I will try to go on is football. As a sophomore, that was my first year ever playing football for a team, besides sandlot. In my junior year, I think I made a huge improvement because I gained more knowledge of the game and gained more strength. I played varsity, and started a few of games. I practiced at line-backer, but ended up playing as a defensive end.

The job of a defensive end is to keep outside containment on the defensive line. When the coach calls defense and your "D" steps onto that field there's only one thing running through your head, "Stop them." You get into your three point stance or position and wait for the snap. When the ball is snapped everything enters slow motion. The game doesn't enter slow motion, but your mind does. As a defensive end, thoughts run through your mind like, "Do I rush inside? Do I keep outside containment? Do I rush the QB? Do I chase the running back? The right decision to listen to is to keep outside containment.

Once the player with the ball runs your way your mind begins to speed up. You square your body and drive through the ball carrier. When you hit him, the collision, the impact is so impulsive, you tackle him to the ground and wait for the referee's whistle. Just to make matters more intense, you look him in the eyes as you rise up from the ground. Then you retrieve to your huddle as if you're superior.

Football to me is organized rugby with equipment. It was created in 1879 by Walter Camp. Thank God for him and his creativity to create such an out-standing sport. I don't remember when I first saw football, but I do remember when I first played it. I was five years old, living in Washington State and it was sandlot football. From that time on I loved the game. I began to watch it on television and take notes. As I got older football helped me to evolve.

In my opinion, I think I have always been good at football. I can't believe it took me five years to get the game into my life. Now, football is my life. I don't think I want to live if I can't play football. Football makes the world go round, and without it there would be no Larry Malone.

If I don't end up playing football it's because God didn't want me to. If football wasn't in my life that doesn't mean my life wouldn't go on. I will continue to live life through my book knowledge from school. I will attend college and receive a bachelor's degree in engineering. I will always and forever love football, but I will always think that could have been me if I don't make it. To answer my own question, "Am I ready?" That would be yes.

CONTRIBUTORS

OLACHI ANAEMEREIBE *plans to study architecture, interior design and business. She dreams of starting her own firm and hopes to keep her modeling talent as a future hobby.*

KARISSA ANDERSON *has high hopes for her future. In addition to developing her gifts for writing and poetry, she will attend college and work to become a pediatrician.*

BRIANNA BARNES *loves numbers and excels at math. She hopes to become a financial analyst and she would love to appear on "Oprah" to share her financial expertise.*

BOBBIE JEAN BARNETT *plans to attend a competitive university where she will study chemical engineering and accounting, and never, ever stop playing her clarinet – even in her sleep.*

MARVIN BELL *received an outstanding musician award and top honors for solo drum competition with a score of "A-One." He plans to continue his family's music legacy.*

JANAE BROTHERS *will attend a four-year college out-of-state. She is considering studying agriculture.*

ALICIA CASTILLO *plans to attend college and study business and hospitality.*

DENIECE CHATMAN *hopes to attend a four-year college to study journalism. She would love to run a wedding planning business and retire to a Tuscan villa, which she has already designed, down to the closet size.*

KENNETH CLARK *dreams of living on the beach. He wants to be a writer, but not full-time, just for fun.*

NELSON DORVLO *plans to attend college and, no matter what anyone says, he will keep playing soccer. He would love to explore the United States and, perhaps return to Ghana for a visit.*

AMANDA ELLIOTT *cannot wait for college where she can answer questions and investigate objects. She dreams of becoming a veterinarian.*

CHRIS FARRAR *plans to attend college at a midwestern university. He hopes to continue to play football.*

ALEXIS FAYNE *hopes to study travel and tourism, or pursue a career in real-estate.*

MISHA FOSTER *will pursue her college studies in the Midwest. She plans to study medicine and continue to write poetry.*

AYRIEL HADLEY *hopes to attend a four-year college and she insists her college will be located in place that is warm! She plans to pursue a degree in engineering.*

GINA JACKSON *wants to pursue a college degree in interior design and the arts. One day she hopes to open her own design firm.*

ALEXIS JAMERISON *plans to attend a four-year college and though she feels she's not so great around kids, she might pursue a degree in education to become a kindergarten teacher.*

MIKE JONES *plans to study accounting at a four-year college. He would love to play college football and professional football in the NFL.*

JASMINE "J.R." JONES *would love to study business at a four-year university to become a real-estate agent, and if the opportunities arise, she'll keep running track.*

JASMINE "JJ" JONES *plans to attend college to pursue a nursing degree and will keep modeling as jobs become available.*

LARRY MALONE *is determined to earn his college degree in engineering. He dreams one day of playing professional football.*

TASHA MCCULLER *plans to attend college on an athletic scholarship. She hopes to become a computer technician.*

DEWAIN M. MEEKS *will go to college and his interests include architecture and sports. He plans to run track in the Olympics and keep on challenging his twin brother, Dwight.*

ERIC OLIVER *plans to pursue a degree in audio engineering. He hopes to use his education and knowledge about music and rap to make a stamp on the hip-hop game.*

LIBBY PAPIAN *plans to attend college in a major metropolitan city where she will pursue a degree in business.*

BRIANA PEPPERS *would love to study science at a four-year college and one day combine her interest in politics with her science degree.*

ASHLEY POLK *would love to continue playing basketball in college if she has the opportunity, but she knows for certain that her future studies will lead her to helping people in need.*

93

CATHERINE "CAT" RUSSELL *hopes to attend a competitive college where she will play basketball and learn Spanish to become a translator.*

TANNER SENTER *will pursue a college education outside of Missouri. He hopes to study law and more than anything in the world, he wants to make a difference.*

DEVON SMALL *would love to study international business, after which he hopes to become rich and famous and change the world for the better.*

JEQUETTA SMITH *plans to attend college to pursue a major in marketing and finance in a business school.*

DEJÁ WHITE *loves singing, God, and her family. She plans to attend a four-year college and follow her dream to become a child psychologist.*

CHRIS WILLIAMS *will pursue his college education at a liberal arts college where he would love to play basketball. He plans to study business and law.*

RANEISHA WILLIAMS *plans to attend a university where she would like to study health management or pre-med, though she is inspired at the possibility of earning a M.D./J.D.*

StudioSTL has been around since May 2005, when seven strangers first met to discuss the feasibility of developing a community-based writing center modeled on the nationally-acclaimed young writer's program in San Francisco, "826 Valencia." The group shared their passion for writing, for kids, for teachers and for the St. Louis community. Many meetings later, the initial group of seven (no longer strangers) unanimously agreed that they would pour their hearts and souls into building a magical, one-of-a-kind, drop-in writing center for students and the St. Louis community.

Today we're moving forward with our mission – WE'RE REACHING KIDS! Imagine seven-year olds penning stories for a miniature dachshund named, Haley, or sixth-graders becoming members of an international press corps with a once-in-lifetime chance to interview the slightly odd and widely unknown, "Sir J.T. Scowling" – an author who, much to the kids' surprise happens to suffer from writer's block? Think poet, writer, AP reporter and illustrator working with thoughts and ideas in front of 250 eighth-graders!

In addition to its in-school programming, StudioSTL has its very own student press corps. The group of 25 journalists published their self-titled, "Tall Tale Truth" in the summer of 2006, which featured exclusive interviews with St. Louis Science Center scientists, former Senator Jean Carnahan and Pat Hagin, owner of The Pageant. The Press Corps and "Tall Tale Truth" will become a regular StudioStL publication with the second issue coming out in the summer, 2007.

The StudioStL community now seeks a permanent site to nurture ideas and imagination, to lend further support to area teachers and youth. The StudioStL writers envision a creative haven of unlimited potential where all are welcome to visit, share stories and create with words – whether in a poem, a film, a cartoon, a book, magazine, newspaper or podcast. With a studio, we will offer student, adult and family writing workshops, field trips, after-school help, drop-in assistance, special writing events, internships and scholarships. The possibilities are endless!

We're in schools. We're mentoring. We're working on student-written publications. And we're downright thrilled at the opportunity to share the power and magic of words with kids.

This book is the first in an anticipated series of long-term StudioStL projects that will bring professional writers, artists, and educators into the classroom to work in partnership with high school students. By working with students over time on topics of interest to them, we hope to build relationships that foster trust and confidence, which we believe are essential to good writing. We offer time, attention, and feedback to help students through all phases of the writing process – from brainstorming to revision – to produce a professional publication that features the students' well-crafted works. The StudioSTL anthology project is modeled on the brilliant work of 826 Valencia, San Francisco.

How It Works
This anthology project took shape in the summer of 2006 when StudioSTL met College Bound. After lots of brainstorming sessions, we decided to collaborate on a book project!

The good people at College Bound allocated weekly classtime with their students at Clyde C. Miller Career Academy and University City High School to StudioStL writing sessions. StudioStL, in turn, sent in its team of writers to work with the College Bound students, beginning in October 2006, each week until January 2007.

We spent our first weeks talking and thinking and getting to know each other. We asked the students to draw, to play with clay, to imagine taking photographs. We brought in live models to show how characters can come to life. (We borrowed this great idea from 826 Valencia.) We talked more. We asked the students to write mini-assignments, but we found that our students had grown to love the conversations and felt a bit reluctant to put pen to page.

Our writers met and discussed the student writing sessions and the stories we heard. We talked with our volunteer teachers and asked them for advice. We kept everything very simple. We agreed that a book was already taking shape – based on the student's stories, the stories they told us in class; stories that changed and became considerably more detailed and rich as the weeks passed and the students got to know us. And, after much time listening and trying to "hear" their stories, we asked the students to write about themselves. We asked them to pen self-portraits. You could have heard more than a pin drop when we broke the news.

Most students despaired. They told us that absolutely nothing about themselves or their lives was interesting. They told us that no one wanted to hear about them and they didn't want to take the time to put anything down. We sensed our students might be holding back. We asked them to answer questions they would ask their friends. We asked lots of questions. What do you want people to know? What's important to you? What do you love? Who inspires you? And then we hit upon one question that seemed to make a difference. We asked them if they felt "judged" and misunderstood. They laughed. So we asked them to consider this thought and to fill in the blank in their own way: "You look at me and think you see one person, but what you really should know is this...."

And then it happened. All of a sudden we saw smiles and we didn't hear many more moans and groans. The students started standing up in class (well, at least one did) and read their work out aloud and sent our writers e-mail and asked for suggestions and called with more details and tried and tried to figure out how to say things that they really wanted to share. Most of all, they asked us whether they could write in their "own way." Most of all, they asked whether what they wrote about was "okay." Most of all, they asked whether what they wrote about was "enough." We said, "Yes."

In February, a volunteer student editorial board met every Sunday to read and review each piece of writing and to offer suggestions for revision. The board offered feedback to each student writer. The student board discussed the book title, talked about the cover design, and what they felt the book meant. They met together – with the StudioSTL writers – each and every week until March, when once again, we heard moans and groans – the end of our student writing sessions.

The students have taught StudioStL much during this writing journey and we feel we have taught them a bit too – about the power of their thoughts and words, and about the necessity of putting things down in a way that will establish connections. We hope that when this brilliant bunch make their way to college – and we know they will with the incredible work of College Bound – we hope the students will feel a bit more confident, now outfitted with a few tips and our applause.

97

Lisa Orden Zarin

My friend Susan Talve told me a story.

She said that in every generation there are 36 righteous souls for whom the whole world stands. No one knows who these 36 are nor do any of the individuals suspect they could be one of them. Outwardly, they are ordinary, flawed and full of imperfections. But their hearts are so pure, their souls so filled with goodness that the whole world continues to exist just because they are in it.

I couldn't get that story out of my head once we recruited our first group of College Bound students.

We had set out to enroll a class of 28 – 30 but after reading the applications, so vulnerable and full of desire, we couldn't whittle down the numbers. We knew it was risky; the organization was young and our budget was slim. But we crossed our fingers, counted out the students who had put their hearts on the line and we enrolled them all. Thirty-six.

We fell in love with them. There were times when we found ourselves unsure of how to rise to the challenges we faced. Our students were so tough and so tender. They resisted us and clung to us. The more we argued with them, the more we became bound up.

St. Louis soon became our classroom. We traveled to museums, theaters, performing arts centers, cafes, universities and lecture halls. We met State Senator Jeff Smith; Post Dispatch writer, Sylvester Brown; Rams Wide Receiver, Isaac Bruce; Secretary of State Colin Powell and Rwandan hero, Paul Rusesabagina, along with many others who gave joyfully of their time and talents.

As I look back at this past year, I think of how audacious we were and on occasion naïve. Some days we were only a baby step ahead of our students and the possibility of failing them kept us up at night. Even though our college counselor, Debbie Greenberg, is one of the finest counselors in St. Louis (and in my opinion one of the finest college counselors who ever walked the earth), there were still times when the challenges felt daunting. But we knew we could not separate from the 36 righteous souls who had placed their trust in us.

So here we are, one year later, more fully human than we were 12 months ago, more awake, more humble and more determined. Occasionally, we meet people who see a group of mostly young black men and women being mentored by a couple of white women. Not infrequently, those encounters are met with suspicion and occasionally outright challenges. "What right do we have thinking that we can teach anything to students who look so different from us?" I nod my head in agreement and tell them the truth, a truth I sensed from the moment we enrolled the 36 students who would become the first class of College Bound.

We're not the teachers here.

ACKNOWLEDGMENTS

This book happened because a group of high school students believed that what they had to say might be important enough to put down in writing. Their work. Their words. Not part of daily curriculum. Not for a grade. Given a hundred different choices about how they might spend their time, these kids chose writing. On their own, in their own way, in their own voice, they shared more of themselves and more of their time than we ever could have imagined. They showed up. For that, we could not be more grateful.

StudioSTL volunteers showed up too – sometimes shouldering moans and raised eyebrows – coaxing, coaching, guiding, sharing, assuring, reassuring, and building trust until "what I really want to write about" emerged. The contribution of this team's talent, wisdom and generosity is truly beyond measure.

The StudioSTL "A-Team"
Cheree Berry
Michele Blanke
Julie Dill
Leslie P. Evans
Nora A. Fitzpatrick
Abby Horne
Joey Lang
Mary O'Malley
Bill Perman
Emily Smith
Jeanne Welling Sabbert Smith
Tess Thompson
Ryan Wheeler

We marveled over Cindy Lappin's remarkable ability to shoot photos of students hunched over their desks. Cindy became invisible at our writing sessions; somehow she and Kevin Vogler captured over 2000 real-life photographs of the students and writers. We remain in awe of Lappin/Vogler Photography and Cindy and Kevin's ability to provide such honest portrayals.

Debbie Greenberg at College Bound coordinated classroom sessions and all imaginable details, including bagels and donuts. Debbie became a fast friend to the StudioSTL writers and made our sessions possible. Likewise, for Lisa Zarin who leads College Bound with enormous heart and extraordinary vision. Ericka Zoll coordinated endless arrangements and meetings.

We "borrowed" Julie Dill, as we often do, from her other book editing duties and from our good friends at Observable Readings. Julie took the pieces and put them together in her always reassuring, always decisive style. We could not manage without Julie.

Mr. Ken Botnick, Washington University, most generously offered to contribute his twenty-five+ years of book design and bookmaking skill and expertise to the first StudioStL student anthology. We are indebted to Ken for his patience and for bringing beauty to the page.

The St. Louis Rams, Alison Collinger, and Tiffani Wilson brought this project to the attention of Mr. Isaac Bruce, who is a hero in St. Louis, not only for his on-the-field achievements, but also for his off-the-field commitment to giving back. Brett Grassumuck fielded phone calls and requests with his usual "can-do" attitude.

Mr. Dick Weiss, WeissWrite LLC, assisted with editing, and he did such a top-notch job, we're secretly hoping that Dick might bring his talents to future StudioSTL student publications.

Mr. Jim Smith, our technology wizard, went above and beyond by easing communication on our e-lists and by creating our first StudioSTL "wiki" for on-line collaboration.

Ms. Leslie Evans copyedited, proofread, and revised text. She is talented and wise beyond her years.

Connie Farrow has supported StudioSTL programming from the beginning. Her special support for this project has earned her a lifetime spot on our special list.

Thanks to the dedicated staff members – security, librarians, educators and administrators at Career Academy and at University City High. A special thank you to Ms. King at Career, who cheerfully located students throughout the day and sent them our way.

Paul Ha, Kathryn Adamchick, and Jennifer Gaby at the Contemporary Art Museum, St. Louis embraced this project as a work of art and generously offered the museum as a site to celebrate publication.

There are certain "sure, no problem" people who are called upon on at a moment's notice, who stay with the kids, who pick up the kids from school, who are the kids who get themselves ready for school, who fix flat tires, who give their weekend time, who offer heaps of praise and support. We acknowledge the contribution of Donna Givens, Mary Greaves, Katy Hawker, Gary Boehnke, and Mary Lou McGuire; Jim Smith, Lydia Smith and Zack Smith; Graham Vogler; John Greenberg, Jason Greenberg, and Elizabeth Greenberg; Jamie Blanke, Ian Blanke and Ellie Blanke; Deb Kraus, Isabel Perman, and Rebecca Perman; Elaine

Marschik; Patricia Yaeger and Ron Bristow, Tony Evans, and Lucas Heberlie; Tom Rodebaugh and Benjamin Thompson Rodebaugh, and Yvonne Skinner.

Among the "sure, no problem" people are three who have earned their own applause. Kate and Jack went to writing sessions, read drafts, encouraged the students and believed. And Brad, who in his quiet way, makes absolutely everything possible.

Thank you.
Elizabeth Ketcher
StudioSTL

For the gift of this book, I would like to thank Beth Ketcher whom I met at the urging of a mutual friend. Over coffee at Kayak's where we met to just chat, we discovered a friendship that would shape the next year of our lives. Maybe it was the caffeine, or the time of day, or just the recognition of a kindred spirit, but in that brief time together, we shared life stories, found similarities in our husbands and children, and revealed to each other our passion: to elevate the lives of young people. By the time we left the café, the idea for a book was sown along with the seeds of a partnership.

For recognizing the importance of this project, I would also like to thank Lisa Orden Zarin, College Bound's Executive Director. Lisa sensed my eagerness to work with StudioStL, and while not every "i" was dotted, she had faith that the book would give our students a "once in a lifetime" experience. That's what makes Lisa so great. With boundless energy, brilliance, and compassion, she wants what's best for our students. She lives and breathes our mission: to provide high potential students with every opportunity to enrich themselves and attain a college education. Ericka Zoll, our development director, was equally excited about the book. I can't thank her enough for lending her energy and talent to this venture and for working her magic to enlist the help of the St. Louis Rams' and ultimately, Isaac Bruce who met with our students and wrote the moving forward to this book.

We can't say enough about the writers of StudioStL whose passion for writing was matched only by their devotion to our students. We are also grateful to Sylvester Brown who launched this project and to the College Bound board who blessed it, Leah Merrifield, Susan Weissman, Flint Fowler, Diane Levine, Robert Bogard, and Harry Orchard. And then there are our students to thank who, after hours of rolling their eyes, got down to the very real and difficult work of writing, revising, laughing, crying, wincing, chuckling, and – finally – celebrating.

Of course, we wouldn't have students with whom to work without the support of the University City School District and the St. Louis City Public School District. Thanks to Joy Lynn Wilson for opening the doors at University City for us. And to principal Elizabeth Bender, assistant principal Dayle Burgdorf, college coordinator Katherine Bailey and administrative assistant Christine Brooks at University City High School. Go, Lions! Thanks also to our partners at Clyde C. Miller Career Academy – principal Stephen Warmack, counselor William Sevier, administrative assistant Toni Russell and loving volunteer, Yvonne Skinner. Go, Phoenix!

Hovering in the wings, and also occasionally wearing them, are the people who have been with College Bound from the beginning. Barrett Toan, Polly O'Brien, Susan Weissman, Kimberly Frost, Orvin Kimbrough, Flint Fowler and Richard D. Baron never stopped encouraging, guiding and cheering us on.

We owe our greatest thanks to our families who continued to support us and applauded our efforts even when there was no food in the refrigerator or gas in the car. To John Greenberg, Larry Zarin, Jason Greenberg, Elizabeth Greenberg, Max Zarin, Carsen Zarin, Aaron Zoll, Adam Zoll, Myrna Meyer, and Jay Meyer, we want you to know that we love and cherish you.

Thanks, lastly, to that earlier-mentioned mutual friend Dena Ladd, who set this project in motion. And to Karen Werner and Tammy Lamb who never fail to put their hearts and talent on the line for College Bound. We are forever in your debt.

Debbie Greenberg
College Bound
April 2007

A note on the design of the book

This book was designed by Ken Botnick with the assistance of Mason Miller at EMDASH studio in St Louis. The text type is Swift designed by Gerard Unger between 1984 and 1987. Titling type is The Sans Regular designed by Luc(as) de Groot as part of the Thesis type family, 1994–99.

106